U0604141

America must know

How to win the heart of others？
How to win without going to war？

By: liu sung tao
(Singaporean)

Bilingual Book

中英文对照

美国应该知道

如何才得人心所向？
如何才能不战而胜？

[新加坡] 刘松涛著

图书在版编目（CIP）数据

美国应该知道 / 刘松涛著. -- 北京 : 九州出版社, 2010.10
ISBN 978-7-5108-0653-7

Ⅰ. ①美… Ⅱ. ①刘… Ⅲ. ①美国对外政策—研究 Ⅳ. ①D871.20

中国版本图书馆 CIP 数据核字（2010）第 176828 号

美国应该知道

作　　者	刘松涛　著
出版发行	九州出版社
出 版 人	徐尚定
地　　址	北京市西城区阜外大街甲 35 号（100037）
发行电话	(010)68992190/2/3/5/6
网　　址	www.jiuzhoupress.com
电子信箱	jiuzhou@jiuzhoupress.com
印　　刷	三河市东方印刷有限公司
开　　本	880 毫米 ×1230 毫米　32 开
印　　张	7.875
字　　数	160 千字
版　　次	2010 年 11 月第 1 版
印　　次	2010 年 11 月第 1 次印刷
书　　号	ISBN 978-7-5108-0653-7
定　　价	28.00 元

美国应该知道

America must know

Preface

There was a Chinese woman who married an American. During their travel to Asia, she warned her children not to admit that they are American for safety reasons. It is to avoid the dire consequence of being beaten up by people who hate Americans.

Being the citizens of a world superpower, and yet having to be so careful and fearful of their traveling abroad, this is really a sad situation for the American! The main reason is because the United States, as a superpower, is doing everything to seek benefits for itself at the expense of others. As a result, there are a lot of people in the world who are unhappy with American foreign policy, including extremist groups that would not hesitate to take retaliatory actions.

In view of this, I have written a collection of constructive proposals in this book for America to consider in implementing its foreign policy. These suggestions were written with the intent to turn hostilities into friendliness and peace, and in the process reduce risk of terrorist attacks. Americans can then be popular again and no longer need to live in an environment fearful of terrorism.

This is my purpose in writing this book, and hopefully it will be able to help the safety of the American.

In addition to the successful publication of this book, first of all I would like to thank the publishers and editorial for their enthusiastic assistance, and thank my family for the understanding and support, giving me the opportunity to come to China to make use the low-cost and professional environment of publication, I would also like to thank sincerely to the following friends and colleagues for their assistance during the publication process, they are: Tay Joo Thong, Wang Wen Qing, Robert Wee, CS.Tay, Li Xiao Di, Ho Fan, Kong Na etc.

前　言

一个嫁给美国人的中国女士到亚洲旅行时告诉她的孩子为了安全，不要承认自己是美国人，以免碰上怀恨美国人的危险分子！

一个世界超强国家的人民，出国旅行时却要如此小心，战战兢兢。这是何等可悲的事情啊！主要原因是由于美国自恃是世界超级强国，可以为所欲为，到处实行损人利己的政策，以致造成很多世人的反感，引起一些极端分子的报复行动。

因此我写了一些有建设性的建议，收集在这本书里。让美国人知道，如果要继续保存世界强国的地位和减少被袭击的危险，应该实行一些争取人心和不战而胜的政策。尽可能化敌为友和世界各国和平相处，使美国人能够到处受人欢迎，不必再生活在防恐、反恐的环境中。

这是我写这本书的目的，但愿能够对美国人的安全生活有所帮助。

另外这本书能够顺利出版，首先我要感谢出版社和编辑部热心的协助，以及感谢我的家人的理解和支持，让我有机会来中国利用这里写书和出书的方便以及低成本的条件。我也要诚心地感谢下列各位朋友和同事在出版过程中的协助，他们是：郑裕通、王文清、李骁迪、何凡、孔娜等。

Contents

目　录

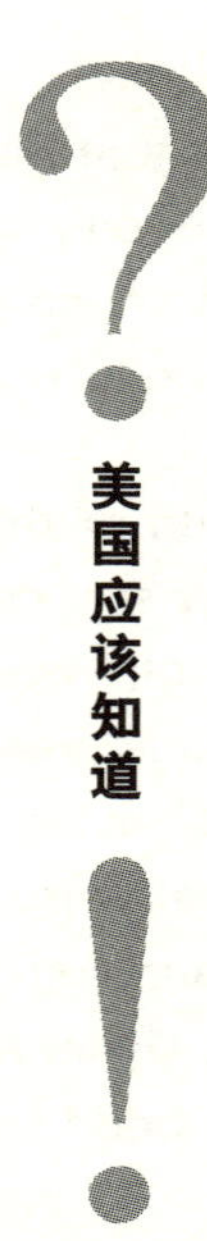

America must know

America, from here to there

Some observers think that after 20-30 years, the United States will remain the world's only superpower, others suggested otherwise. Judging from the current situation, it is hard for the USA to remain the most powerful nation unless there is a change in its policy!

The reason the wealth of the United States has been depleted by its huge military spending and the two wars of Iraqi and Afghanistan. The country is incurring more debt by the days! Though the President is preaching "spend less and save more", the Government could not reduce its budget deficit. Lower consumption means a weaker market economy and a direct impact on unemployment and negative returns on home equity for more and more people. Under such circumstances, can the United States remain the world's only super power in 20-30 years?

Things will develop in the opposite direction when they become extreme, therefore the United States should be contented of its status and strive to maintain itself as a world's super power or one of the super power by perhaps considering the following policies:

1. The US should withdraw its military presence in Japan and South Korea since they are not welcome by the people of Japan and South Korea. Japan's new policy has clearly demonstrated that they will not assist the U.S. in its hegemony of Asia. A military withdrawal could prompt an early reunification of North and South

美国何去何从？

有些观察家认为20~30年后美国仍然是世界上唯一的超级强国，也有人认为不尽然：以目前的国际情况，美国如果不改变政策，20~30年后最多只能是世界上一个强国之一而已，再没办法唯我独尊了！

理由是美国的财富已经被巨大的军事开销和伊拉克及阿富汗两场战争拖垮了！国家的债务越来越多！政府的赤字有增没减，总统虽然主张“少消费，多储蓄”，但能做得到吗？少消费将造成市场萎缩，经济不能复苏！失业和负资产的人越来越多。要如何多储蓄呢？在这种情况之下，20~30年后，美国还能够保持世界唯一强国的地位吗？

所谓物极必反，美国应该懂得知足，适可而止，要争取在20~30年后仍是世界强国之一的地位，也许应该考虑实行下列一些新的政策：

1. 既然日本和韩国的人民都不欢迎美国的驻军，就应该全部收兵回营，反正日本的新政策已经显示不会协助美国在亚洲称霸了，把驻韩国美军和对准朝鲜的核武撤走，可能促使其早日统一，以便消除美国对朝鲜核武器的担心，也可以节省驻外军队的开销，争取世人的好感，一举数得，何乐而不为呢？

2. 欧洲几十个国家已经组成了强大的欧盟，他们的安全绝对不需要美国的保护了，把驻欧的美军全部撤退不但可以节省大量在外驻军的开销，也可以因此而取得与俄罗

Korea, remove the treat of North Korea's nuclear weapons and save on the cost of the armed forces stationed abroad. A win-win situation!

2. Dozens of countries in Europe have joined forces for a formidable EU. Their security is beyond the need of a protection from the United States. A complete withdrawal not only saves on huge military spending but encourages a cordial relationship with Russia. This is perhaps the best US policy to be taken in Europe.

3. Abolish US-Taiwan Act. Be an active supporter for the peaceful unification of China and Taiwan. With the strength of 1.3 billion Chinese consumer markets, a healthy friendship with China will enable President Obama to achieve his goal on capturing the Asian market.

4. The US should refer all international disputes to the United Nations and not take unilateral action to protect its own interest. Assist UN in getting stronger and more powerful in its peacekeeping task.

5. To Prevent indirect problems for the world, the United States should change its stance on suppression of terrorism. Jesus said "Love your enemies"; revenge will bring more misery to oneself. Americans should learn from the late President Eisenhower; never waste a minute thinking about people we don't like".

21st December, 2009

斯的和平相处。这也许是美国应该在欧洲采取的上策。

3. 取消美国《与台湾关系法》，主动支持中国的和平统一，换取13亿中国人的巨大市场和长远的友谊也能够为美国货在亚洲找到大买家，这也符合奥巴马总统要打开亚洲市场的愿望。

4. 协助联合国组织实力强大的维和部队，把一切有关美国利益的任何国际纠纷全交付联合国处理，解决因采取单边行动而造成吃力不讨好的伤害。

5. 美国应该改变防恐、反恐的立场，不要为世界制造间接的麻烦，记住耶稣的圣言“爱你的敌人”，不要试图去报复仇敌，以免伤害到自己甚于敌人的伤害。美国人应该学习已故总统艾森豪威尔的做法，“不要把时间浪费在去想那些我们不喜欢的人。”

写于2009年12月21日

⊙ 洛杉矶举行反战大游行

The high cost of getting even

On September 11, 2001 two landmark building in New York were destroyed by Al-Qaeda extremists using U.S. civilian aircrafts. Thousands of innocent lives were lost in this incident. This brutal tragedy took place unexpectedly in a major city of the world superpower, the United States of America. It was carried out by 19 non-militant Al-Qaeda men. It caused such serious damage that the Americans felt deeply saddened. It came as a great surprise to the world!

The United States condemn 9/11 incident as an act of terrorist war crime, rather than individual activists. In retaliation, the U.S. dispatched 150,000 strong army to attack and kill the so-called head of terrorist groups in Iraq and their leader, Mr. Saddam Hussein! It cost the United States nearly one trillion U.S. dollars in military spending, and thousands of soldiers' lives. Yet, it did not lead to a pro-American Iraqi government. The American people are still without a sense of security in Iraq resulting in lots of oil field development rights to others foreign companies!

Concurrent to the war in Iraq, the United States dispatched more than 30,000 troops to Afghan and provided generous awards to local Afghan in searching for Osama bin Laden, aiming at eliminating al-Qaeda's activities. After eight years of tough war, the US was unable to achieve its original goal. The US could not even obtain reliable intelligence of Osama Bin Laden hideout, let alone catching him. This is mainly due to the lack of support from the local people! Hundreds of billions onwar spending were

报复的代价太高了!

2001 年 9 月 11 日纽约两座地标大厦被基地组织的极端分子利用美国民航飞机给撞毁了！同时夺去了几千个无辜的生命。这样残酷的突发事件，竟然发生在这个世界超强国家的大都市，对美国来说，实在是奇耻大辱。基地组织只用了 19 个非军人的行动，就给美国造成了如此严重的伤害，令美国人感到极度的悲愤，也使全世界人民大吃一惊！

美国认定 911 事件本质是恐怖战争而不是个别犯罪分子的活动，为了报复，美国出动了 15 万大军，首先针对所谓恐怖集团的大本营，把伊拉克和其领导人萨达姆干掉！但美国付出的代价是近万亿美元的军事开支，以及几千条军人的性命，结果还换不来一个亲美国的伊拉克政府，美国人民在伊拉克仍没有安全感，以致美国石油公司对伊拉克油田的开发裹足不前，全给外国公司拿去了！真是情何以堪！

在攻打伊拉克的同时美国出动了 3 万多军队和提供了丰厚的偿金给阿富汗当地官兵协助搜捕本·拉登和消除基地组织的活动。但经历了 8 年的艰苦战争，仍无法实现最初的目标，不但捉不到本·拉登，连他的藏身之处也没有可靠的情报，主要是输在民心！白费了几千亿美元的战争开支。

不断主张要从阿富汗撤军的奥巴马总统最近也只好面

wasted!

The US president Obama is a major advocate of withdrawal from Afghanistan, however, he ends up with no other choice but to accept the reality of sending more troops to Afghanistan. The surge also came with direct results of increased military spending. The U.S. government is estimated to have spent more than one million US dollars per year for every soldier stationed in Afghanistan. Base on a total of 100,000 troops, the future of the Afghanistan war will cost as high as 100 billion U.S. dollars per year.

No wonder the majority of heavyweight Democrats has issued a joint statement to the House of Representatives suggesting levying a “war tax in Afghanistan”. If implemented, I am afraid the American people will have to pay the war tax indefinitely without an end in the near future. It’s unconceivable that this could have happened to a world super-power!

When the war ended, the Afghan government may want to claim from the U.S. government compensation on damages caused by the war against Al-Qaeda and Taliban. Therefore, the results of the war in Afghanistan are a double barrel loss of money and soldiers for the American. Nevertheless, Osama bin Laden and Al-Qaeda may be still there, the internal security threat to the United States is still unresolved. These two retaliation war are “High Cost of Getting Even” for the American. They should study China’s policy of “harmony” instead.

17th, December, 2009

对现实决定对阿富汗增兵。但增兵的结果军事开支也将再次相应增加，据说美国政府必须每年为每位驻阿士兵付出100万美元以上的战争费用，如果以10万军人计算，则未来的阿战费每年将高达1000亿美元以上。

难怪美国众议院多数重量级民主党议员已经发表联合声明，建议要为阿富汗战争向人民征收“阿富汗战争税”，如果真的实行，美国人民今后恐怕要不断缴纳战争税了！这样的事情不应该发生在一个世界超级强国上。

阿富汗战争结束后，美国政府可能还要应对阿富汗政府的赔偿要求，因为美国对塔利班基地组织的战争，给阿富汗政府和人民造成严重的损失，也应该为他们支付一笔合理的战后费用。因此，美国在阿富汗战争的结果可能是“赔了金钱又折兵”。本·拉登捉不到，基地组织依然存在，对美国国内安全的威胁仍然没有清除，这两场报复的战争付出的代价太大了！美国应该学中国“以和为贵”的政策。

写于2009年12月17日

⊙ 美国“持久自由”反恐军事行动在阿拉伯海湾举行

Obama deep bow worth

President Barack Obama made a 90 degree deep bow to the Japanese emperors during his visit to Japan in November 2009. This has caused many Americans to complain that the deep bow to Japan's emperor Akihito was out of the norm, a little too servility of manners seems to have damaged the character of a great nation. As a U.S. president, he should not kneel down to any country's leader!

Obama, in particular the depth of bow to the Japanese emperor's either intentionally or unintentionally, not only caused resentment from his people, some arrogant westerners also feels uncomfortable by what Obama did! In any case, I believe that the deep bow of president Obama to the Japanese emperor may have its purpose. He may do it for the country's interest at the expense of his own dignity; people should understand his pain.

President Obama has repeatedly pointed out that the America can't rely solely on military and economic super power, the trend of people are equally important to influent the world. Therefore Obama is determined to pursue a "smart power" policy: he knew that the elements of the Japan Democratic Party won the election because the major Japanese voters were supporting their "distance U.S. and closer to Asia" policy.

The clever president Obama knew that in order to make Japanese Democratic Party to change their policy forward America, he must first of all strive for Japanese voters to favor the United States and the best way to achieve this is to pay respect

奥巴马的鞠躬值得!

2009年11月美国总统奥巴马访日期间向日本天皇90度深鞠躬，引起很多美国人的不满，认为美国总统如此鞠躬的姿势和日皇又鞠躬又握手的举止显得有点卑躬屈膝，有降低国格之嫌。美国总统不应该对任何国家的领袖有如此低身下气的举动！

奥巴马对日皇的深度鞠躬，不管是有意或无意，不但会引起其国民的反感，相信一些向来骄傲自大的西方人也有物伤其类的感受。不管如何，我相信奥巴马对日皇谦恭的姿态，是有其目的的，他可能为了其国家的利益，而牺牲自己的尊严，人民应该对他的苦心加以理解。

奥巴马总统一再指出，当今的世界单靠军事和经济的超强力量，美国已经不能单独领导这个世界了！他决心要实行“软外交政策”，人心的趋向更为重要。日本民主党能够胜选执政，是因为日本选民支持他们的轻美重亚的政策，民主党许诺当选后要和美国重新谈判驻军问题，在国际外交方面要有自主权，民主党提倡的东亚共同体，也表明了不欢迎美国参与。

因此聪明的奥巴马总统为了使民主党能够回心转意，继续与美国结盟，首先必须争取日本选民对美国的好感，而对日皇表示特别尊敬就是对症下药的好办法，因为大部分日本人民对日皇仍是忠心耿耿的。

日本一个网民这样写道：“奥巴马总统对日皇如此尊敬

to the Japanese emperor. Because of most Japanese are still very loyal to their emperor.

A Japanese writer wrote: "never before has any U.S. president respected Japanese emperor as president Obama, his attitude and his manner made me feel so good".

From the well praise of the Japanese people toward president Obama, we can see the sacrifice of his dignity is worthwhile, his soft policy is correct, the hard line policy of Japanese Democratic toward the U.S. may thus be loosen.

For the interest of USA, Congress members who frequently make irresponsible remarks on China's affairs should learn from president Obama's "bow" action in order to obtain the good will of the Chinese.

30th, November, 2009

的态度是以前任何美国总统做不到的，他的亲切举止使我感觉很好……”

从日本人民对奥巴马总统的好评就可以知道他的“软外交政策”是对的，他牺牲的尊严是有价值的，日本民主党轻美的政策可能因此而有所松动。

美国国会一些经常对中国国情说三道四的议员，应该学习奥巴马总统的“鞠躬”动作，才能获得中国人的好感。

写于 2009 年 11 月 30 日

⊙ 美国举办灯笼会纪念广岛原子弹爆炸中的死难者

US not leaving Asia

The United States never said that they wanted to leave Asia; they also knew that they must continue to remain in Asia, in order to balance China's economic and military growing power.

When the United States executed friendship treaty with the Association of South East Asian Nations, observers commented that: "It was a strong signal that the United States is willing to deepen relations with ASEAN in order to counter China's growing influence in ASEAN." Hillary Clinton Secretary of State repeatedly stressed that the United States will not abandon Asia during the signing ceremony.

When the Japanese Minister of Foreign Affairs mentioned that the United States should not be involved in the East Asian community organization, the Assistant Secretary of Pacific Affairs also immediately responded that "At present in Asia, the dominant mechanism is not clear, but any things involved in important mechanism like economic, security, business should include the United States."

Obviously, the United States are well aware of it will risk losing the leaderships of the world if they do not remain in Asia. Many people think that in 20-30 years, the U.S. will remain the world's only superpower country, this may be an undeniable fact, but we need to remind the United States, to become a true powerful country first of all you need to win the heart of major people of the world.

Therefore, if the United States wishes to be more welcome,

美国没想要离开亚洲

美国从来没说过要离开亚洲，美国也知道他必须继续留在亚洲，以便平衡中国在经济和军事上的崛起。

当美国与东盟签立友好协约时，观察家就指出：“这是一个强烈的信号，说明美国愿意深化与东盟的关系，以便对付中国在东盟越来越大的影响力。”希拉里国务卿在签约时也一再强调美国是不会放弃亚洲的。

当日本外务大臣主张美国不应该参与东亚共同体时，负责太平洋地区事务的助理国务卿坎贝尔马上表态说：“目前亚洲地区的主导机制并不明确，但任何可能涉及安全、经济、商业的重要机制，美国一定要参与。”

很明显地美国已深知如果它离开亚洲，将会失去领导世界的危险，不必经由任何人的提醒。很多人认为在20~30 年内美国仍将是世界唯一的超强国家，这也许是无可否认的事实，但我们必须提醒美国，只有人心所向才能成为真正的强国。

因此，美国如果要得到更多亚洲人的欢迎，也许应该考虑实行下列几点有益于亚洲的新政策：

1. 既然美国感觉到要对付中国的崛起是“说易行难”，那就应该和中国合作，利用中国崛起的能力，共同协助亚洲各国，使他们都能够发展得更快更好。

2. 不要强求亚洲各国都能够像美国一样实行自由民主的政策，应该求同存异，允许有不太自由和不太民主的政

by Asians it should consider implementing the following policies for the benefit of Asians:

1. Since America felt to stop the China's growing power is "easier said than done", then why not cooperate with them to make use of China's rising resources together to help other Asia countries to be able to develop faster and better.

2. Do not insist that all Asia countries must adopt America freedom and democracy policy, allowed common ground while reserving differences on minor ones, to prove that a free and democratic system is worthy of praise.

3. Before the incomes and living standards of Asians can keep up with Americans, U.S. should not force Asia people to pay too high copy rights for American cultural products like computer software, films and music discs etc. The production house should be willing to make less profit in order to sell at much lower price, to let more Asian people to be able to enjoy of America's cultures products. This is one of the great ways to win the world without the war.

4. To take truth action to help Asian countries quell all their disputes peacefully to prove that "the U.S. is Asia's peace-maker" rather than "trouble-maker" in order to obtain more favorable impression of Asians.

11th, November, 2009

府存在，才能显得自由民主的可贵。

3. 在亚洲人的收入和生活水平未能跟上欧美人之前，不要强迫亚洲人以昂贵的价格购买美国的电脑软件、电影及音乐等光碟，应该以薄利多销的政策让更多的亚洲人可以享受到更多的美国文化，才容易达到不战而胜的目的。

4. 以实际行动协助亚洲各国平息所有纠纷以便证明“美国是亚洲和平制造者”而不是“麻烦制造者”，以此取得更多亚洲人的好感。

写于 2009 年 11 月 11 日

⊙ 美国前国务卿赖斯出席博鳌国际旅游论坛并发表演讲

Japan has changed!

In my previous blog, I have constantly reminded the United States that: do not use Japan to contain China. Japan will sooner or later estrange the United States to be closer to China. The United States should stop supporting Taiwan's independence and the separation of Tibet and Xinjiang in exchange for China's better friendship and gain more benefits.

It can finally confirm that my prediction is correct now. The ruling democratic party of Japan, after winning their votes making announcement, immediately, that they would like to talk to the United States for equal relationship. Also it decided to stop provide oil services to the U.S. war in Afghanistan and actively advocated the establishment of an East Asian community with the China and South Korea and do not want America to participate.

The assistant secretary of Pacific Affairs stated his position that: "at present in Asia the dominant mechanism is not clear. But any things involved important mechanism in security, economic, business should include the United States. The United States is an active molecule. We will participate in it."

"We will participate in it" What a super power customary tone! But Katsuya Okada the Japanese foreign minister insists that "East Asian community is a participant of China, Japan, South Korea, Asia, India, Australia, and New Zealand. East Asian community should not include the United States. He said that, if with the United States it means half of the world will be involved and it will not very decent! Let the United States do what it wants

日本变了！

我以前的博客，曾经不断地提醒美国不要利用日本牵制中国，日本迟早会疏远美国而靠近中国的，美国应该停止支持“台独”、“藏独”、“疆独”，以换取中国更好的友谊，更多的利益。

现在终于可以证实我的预言正确了，日本民主党胜选执政后，马上宣布要和美国争取平等的关系，同时决定不再为在阿富汗战争的美军提供供油服务，并积极主张和中国、韩国成立东亚共同体，而且不欢迎美国参与。

负责太平洋地区事务的助理国务卿坎贝尔在北京表态说：“目前亚洲地区的主导机制并不明确，但任何涉及安全、经济、商业的重要机制都不应该将美国置之在外，美国是一个活跃分子，我们会参与其中。”

“我们会参与其中”而不是我们要求参与其中，这可能是超级大国的习惯性语气，但日本外相冈田克也的反应也不再是弱者，他直率地表示：“东亚共同体的参加国是中国、日本、韩国、东盟、印度、澳大利亚、新西兰。东亚共同体不应该包括美国，他说要是加上美国，那不就等于世界的一半了？这样会很不像样！让美国自己搞自己的吧！”

几十年来，日本是美国在亚洲的最忠诚盟国，如今美国突然间听到这么逆耳的话，不知道有何感想。

其实如果让日本、韩国和中国成立共同体携手合作、

to do by themselves."

For decades, Japan is America's most loyal allies in Asia and now the United States suddenly is faced with such an unpleasant situation. I do not know how America can take it. In fact, if let Japan, South Korea and China establish the East Asia community together and join efforts to promote the progress of the 10 Asian countries, make them coexist peacefully. America will no longer need to worry about the security of Japan and South Korea. By then all the arms forces station there, can be withdrawn and save huge military cost for the United States.

As to the economic and commercial interest, naturally it will benefit the parties in proximity. America should not be so brooding.

20th, October, 2009

出钱出力，推动东盟10国的进步，和平相处，日本和韩国的安全就不必美国担心，驻在日本和韩国的军队也可以全部撤退，省下巨大的军事费用，这是目前美国最需要做的事。

至于经济和商业上的利益，所谓近水楼台先得月，美国何必耿耿于怀呢？

写于2009年10月20日

⊙ 日本努力开发旅游业吸引各国游客

Peace Keeping Troops

The Norwegian Nobel committee on 9 October, 2009 awarded the 2009 Nobel peace prize to the U.S. president Barack Obama. Surprising the international community expressed different comments positive and negative opinions.

The Taliban in Afghanistan said: Obama should have got a "Nobel prize of violence".

Iran said: "the U.S. president after winning the Nobel peace prize should put more efforts to make himself a real peace maker."

Iraqi Aoerkazha Lane said: "he is not qualified to receive this award all America made problems in Iraq. Afghanistan has not been solved. The man with slogan of changing has not made any changes."

Obama winning is more symbolic and for imaging. More results are needed from him. Obama in the diplomat front has made many positive efforts. The biggest bright spot is the denuclearization and the efforts to improve relation with the Islam's world, Russia, Cuba, Venezuela, Iran and other countries to ease the tension. They also decided to give up the missile defense plans in Eastern Europe. These could be his wining scores.

In addition to the international award-winning big surprise for Obama, but also reflects some concern for Obama' diplomacy in addition to suspect that Obama can implement his promise of beauty. But the Obama administration's trade projectionist

设立“和平”部队

挪威诺贝尔委员会10月9日把2009年度诺贝尔和平奖授予美国总统贝拉克·奥巴马，令不少国际人士大感意外，纷纷提出正反双面的评论。

阿富汗塔利班嘲弄说：“奥巴马应该拿‘诺贝尔暴力奖’。”

伊朗方面说：“美国总统获得诺贝尔和平奖后应该更加努力使自己‘名副其实’。”

伊拉克人奥尔卡扎里说：“他现在不配获得这个奖，所有美国制造的问题——伊拉克、阿富汗问题都没得到解决，这个以变革为口号的人还没做出什么变革。”

奥巴马的获奖较多是象征意义和想象成分，而尚未看到其他成效。奥巴马上任以来在外交方面的确做出许多积极努力，最大亮点是在无核化方面的努力，改善与伊斯兰世界的关系，和俄罗斯、古巴、委内瑞拉及伊朗等国缓和关系，尝试化敌为友，放弃在东欧设置反导计划也得分不少。从这些角度看奥巴马得奖是在情理之中。

国际上对奥巴马获奖除了大感意外之外，也反映出人们对奥巴马外交的一些忧虑，除了怀疑奥巴马能否落实他的美丽诺言之外，奥巴马政府的贸易保护主义倾向也十分引人关注，一些观察家认为和平奖颁给奥巴马有故意无视其贸易保护主义倾向之嫌。而这种倾向对全球经济的恢复乃至世界和平都将产生难以估量的危害。例如：最近对中

tendencies is also very concern some observers believe that Obama has deliberately ignore its trade protectionist tendencies in Newcastle and this tendency on the global economic recovery and world peace will have immeasurable harm. For example, a recent entry announced that china's tire-dumping will face a heavy import duty that would trigger a chain of effect. The U.S. user will pay higher import duty. Rubber market will go down, the rubber plantation will suffer. China may also raise some U.S. imported produces duty against the U.S. protectionist policy.

Obama himself also "surprised by the deep feeling of embarrassment he will take this honor as spur actions."

However, to achieve as a peace maker president. Much first of all to win the confidence in the world and to quell the negative criticism president Obama might have to create a "peace department and appoint a full time" peace minister. Spend money and effort and changing the mandate of the exiting oversea military into a "peace keeping armed forces" to help eliminate all kind of disputes between states to states to make a real contribution for lasting peace in the world.

12th, October, 2009

国轮胎入口宣布征收倾销税的措施，将会引发连锁反应，美国用户将会因为轮胎起价而影响其业务，国际胶价大跌使种植人吃亏，中国可能也会对部分美国入口货提高入口税，对抗美国的保护主义。

奥巴马本人也“感到很意外，深感受之有愧”，说将把这个荣誉当作行动的鞭策。

要做到名副其实的和平总统，提高世人对他的信心，平息反面的批评，奥巴马总统也许应该成立一个专职的“和平部门”，委任一个“和平部长”，出钱出力将驻守在世界各地的美国军队改变任务，负责搞好世界和平工作，改称为“和平部队”，协助消除国与国之间大小纠纷，为世界的持久和平做出真正的贡献。

写于 2009 年 10 月 12 日

⊙ 奥巴马获诺贝尔和平奖

America Olympic Bid failed

America Olympic bid failed on 2nd October 2009. The plenary session of the international Olympic committees held in Danish Capital-Copenhagen voted Rio de Janeiro of Brazil to hold the 2016 summer Olympic Games.

The four candidate cities were Chicago, Madrid, Tokyo and Rio de Janeiro. Competition was fierce. All of them had sent their heavy weights delegation including head of states.

The U.S. president and his wife also attended the voting campaign. But it didn't help. Chicago was out on the first round voting because got only 18 votes out of 96 and Tokyo was eliminated in the second round of voting. The Rio de Janeiro got the majority votes in the third round to win over against the Madrid of Spain.

The results of Olympic voting indicated two things:

First: The world seems to be more rational now. The most committee members voted according to their own choice and not influenced by the large country.

Second: The world super power countries seem no longer able to summon wind and rain and do whatever they like. Unpopular policy will be cast aside.

The crusades of the U.S. president could not win even sympathy votes. But the cause of Chicago's unsuccessful attempt on the first round voting may be because of him. What unbearable embarrassment!

The president should think over after this disappointment

美国申奥失败！

2009 年 10 月 2 日美国申奥失败了。国际奥委会第 121 届全会在丹麦首都哥本哈根投票决定：巴西——里约热内卢获得 2016 年夏季奥运会主办权。

此次申奥竞争空前激烈，四个候选城市为美国的芝加哥、西班牙的马德里、日本的东京和巴西的里约热内卢。各候选城市都搬出包括国家首脑在内的重量级人物。

美国总统和夫人破例亲自出席拉票，但第一轮投票结果显示，芝加哥因为得票最少，成为第一个出局的城市！因为在总数 96 票中只获得了 18 张支持票。东京也相继在第二轮投票中被淘汰，巴西的里约热内卢在第三轮投票中以绝对多票数击败西班牙的马德里而胜出。

这次奥运会主办权的竞争结果说明了两件事：

第一，世界各国变得比较有理性了！申奥结果显示各国似乎都能依照自己的意见投票，不太受大国影响了！

第二，世界富强国家似乎不能再呼风唤雨、随心所欲了！不得人心的政策将被人唾弃！

这次美国总统“御驾亲征”，不但争取不到同情票，反而使芝加哥沦为第一个出局的城市！简直不可思议，阴沟里翻船，情何以堪！

总统先生失望之余，也许应该加以检讨，为什么美国在世界上拥有那么多的友好盟国，平时为他们出钱出力，保护他们的安全和利益，但在申奥投票时却得不到应得的

why America had spent so much money and looked after so many friendly allies' countries in the world. But can't get enough support. Really, if this can be endured what could not be! It's time for America to review its global policy.

This unexpected failure of the United States may be attributed to the following points:

1. In order to guard against terrorist legislation thorough investigation of cross-boundary passenger, including personal computers has to be detained for the security checking with these troublesome procedures made people feel should kept Chicago away from the Olympic Games.

2. More and more countries unhappy with America super power countries attitude even some friendly allies become strange bedfellows, do not cast votes in Chicago

3. The United States policy is still conceited: ignore the feeling of outsiders, for example America often claims that she wants to be friendly and cooperate with China. But on the other hand continue to cause trouble for China on Taiwan, Tibet and Xinjiang issues. She refused to win the goodwill of 1.3 billion Chinese people in exchange for better interest of the United States including possibility of votes in Chicago bid?

9th, October, 2009

支持！真是：是可忍，孰不可忍！美国调整全球政策的时候到了！

美国这次遭遇到意想不到的失败，可能要归咎于下列几点：

1. 美国为了提防恐怖分子，立法严查出入境旅客，包括可以扣留私人电脑加以检查的麻烦手续，使人们觉得应该对芝加哥敬而远之。

2. 不喜欢美国的国家越来越多，连一些友好的盟国也同床异梦，不投芝加哥的票！

3. 美国外交政策，依然唯我独尊，不太理会外人的感受。例如对中国，口口声声说要友好合作，但对台湾、西藏和新疆问题，仍不断为中国制造麻烦。不衡量轻重得失，不肯博取13亿中国人的好感，以换取美国可得的更好利益！包括为芝加哥申奥拉票的可能性。

写于2009年10月9日

⊙ 两千亚裔举办支持芝加哥2016申奥造势晚会

Trouble-maker to Peace-maker

The United States has agreed to talk with North Korea face to face in order to persuade North Korea to return to six-party talks regarding the nuclear test issue.

My previous blog where I had reminded the United States that to resolve the North Korea nuclear test problems it should be counting on the possibility of reunification for the South and North Korea. Take the reunification of Germany as an example, the poverty and backwardness of the East Germany with the prosperity and progress in West Germany... after the reunification all of the country people can enjoy a life of civilization and progress.

Thus the United States and North Korea bilateral talk should not worry so much whether North Korea immediately accepts a cessation of nuclear test. Instead US should patiently advise North Korea that for the good of the Korean people North Korea should consider first of all unification with the South, taking the unification of Germany as an example where peace and prosperity results after unification. People will naturally want peace not war! The nuclear test problem can be overcome easily.

If the United States can take this bilateral talks opportunity to persuade North Korea to shelve its nuclear test issue and consider to unify of north and south seriously and to ensure the North Korea will be able to get the most favorable conditions.

By the assistance of the United States on this matter the US not only need no longer worry about North Korea's nuclear test

由麻烦制造者到和平制造者

美国改变对朝鲜的立场，同意与朝鲜面对面通过双边会晤，劝说朝鲜重返六方会谈。

我在以前的博客里，曾经提醒美国要解决朝鲜核试的问题，应该寄望于韩国和朝鲜统一。以东西德统一为例子，贫穷落后的东德和富裕进步的西德，统一后全国人民可同样享受着文明进步的生活，就会安分守己地融入世界大家庭了！

因此，美国和朝鲜的双边会谈，不必太着重于朝鲜是否能够马上接受停止核试的结果，以免被朝鲜所开的“天价”惊退！不欢而散。应该耐心地引导和劝告朝鲜，必须以韩国和朝鲜的统一问题为重。以东德人领导目前的德国为例，韩国和朝鲜统一后，朝鲜的领袖，如果有本事，也可以领导整个统一后的韩国。利用韩国在经济上的成就，科技上的进步，把韩国经营得更好。能够使朝鲜人民可以和韩国人民共同享受富裕的成果，人们就自然要和平，而不要战争了！核试问题也可以迎刃而解。

美国如果能利用这次双边会谈的机会，说服朝鲜搁置核试问题，先谈韩国和朝鲜统一的事，保证为朝鲜争取有利的统一条件。

在美国的协助下，如果能够使韩国和朝鲜早日统一，美国不但不必再为朝鲜的核试问题伤脑筋，也可以摘掉朝

issue but also can make America become a Korean peninsula peace-maker and no longer as trouble maker in the region. This is a new policy that is worthwhile for America leaders to consider.

14th, September, 2009

鲜半岛麻烦制造者的恶名，变为和平制造者，这是很值得美国政府领导人加以考虑的新政策。

写于 2009 年 9 月 14 日

⊙ 朝核问题

Japan Reminded US

The leader of Democratic Party of Japan Yuki Hatoyama published an article in the United States prior to his victory to present their position on the Japan-US relationship. He clearly reminded the American government that "if we are elected to power, the future of Japan's national strategy should focus on how to maintain Japan's national interests in between the two countries, while dedicate to achieve a more equitable Japan-US relation. They would also seek for developing relationships with China and other Asian countries.

Yuki Hatoyama also said that "Japan-US security treaty will remain the cornerstone of Japan's foreign policy. But we must remember that our rational identity in Asia. I believe the increasingly show signs of dynamism in East Asia must be regarded as the basis of Japan's geographical presence".

Turning to America's global status, Hatoyama wrote that "with the failure of the Iraq war and financial crisis, the US-led globalization is moving toward the end. The world will usher in a multiplier era. But the next two to three decades, the United States will continue to maintain military and economic leadership."

Given the US influence is declining while China's influence is growing, he stressed that "the future of Japan's national strategy should focus on how to maintain the Japan national interests in between the two countries.

Therefore, when the US policy in Asia conflict with the Japan national interests, the new government of Japan may not be able

日本提醒美国

日本民主党党首鸠山由纪夫在没有胜选之前，曾在美国发表一篇文章介绍其日美关系的立场。他明确地提醒美国政府："如果他当选执政，未来的日本国家战略应着眼于如何在两者之间维护日本的国家利益，寻求实现更为平等的日美关系，同时致力于发展与中国和亚洲其他国家的关系。"

鸠山由纪夫亦表示，"日美安保条约仍将是日本外交政策的基石，但同时我们必须记住我们的亚洲国家身份，我相信日益显示活力的东亚，必须被视为日本的地缘存在基础。"

在谈及美国全球地位时，鸠山写道："由于伊拉克战争的失败和金融危机，美国主导的全球化正在走向终结，世界将迎来多极化的时代，但今后二三十年内，美国仍将在军事和经济上保持领先地位。"

鉴于美国的影响力正在衰落，而中国的影响力日益增强。"他强调："未来日本国家战略应着眼于如何在两者之间维护日本国家的利益。"

因此，当美国的亚洲政策和日本的国家利益有冲突时，日本对美国的立场就不会和以往一样唯命是从了！

美国应该好自为之，抢先和中国建立真正的友好关系

to obey anymore!

In view of this the United States should be careful and the best of all is to establish truly friendly relationships with China as early as possible. If let Japan to embrace China alone the world of Asia may belong to the Japan and China!

7th, September, 2009

才是上策。如果让日本单独拥抱中国，亚洲就将是中日的世界了！

写于 2009 年 9 月 7 日

⊙ 奥巴马视察太阳能公司时表示不愿意美国丢掉领先地位

What US could offer ASEAN

The United States has signed the treaty of amity and cooperation with the Association of South-east Asian Nations (ASEAN) recently.

The treaty commits signatories to three basic principles: peaceful settlement of disputes, non-recourse to the use of force and non-interference of domestic affairs.

These three principles in fact are disadvantageous to the United States; as such Washington has been reluctant to sign the non-aggression pact for years. She is concerned that she has little room to exert its influence on political and security issues in the region.

China has emerged as a key trading partner with ASEAN. And growing in global power later. American then realizes that to sign the pact with ASEAN is necessary. Observers said "by signing this friendship pact with ASEAN the United States sends a strong signal of its desires to deepen ties and counter China's increasing influence."

But how to counter China's influence in ASEAN? It could be a tough job for the US secretary of State Hillary Clinton to brain storm! ...since America has in financial and economic big problems. So financial aid and open free market like China to ASEAN is out of the question.

What methods can America consider to influence ASEAN is the America cultural production like: computer software, movies, music and other expensive copy right products that most ASEAN

美国能够为东盟提供什么?

最近，美国和东南亚组织协会（东盟）签署了友好协约。

该协约有三项承诺的基本原则：和平解决争端，不寻求武力协助，以及不干涉他国内政。

事实上这三个原则是不太符合美国的利益的，因此，华盛顿一直不太乐意签署这个互不侵犯条约，担心这将会失去美国在这个地区的政治和安全影响力。

只有当中国已经成为东盟的重要贸易伙伴，成为不断增长的全球力量，美国才觉得有必要与东盟签立这个协约。有观察家指出："美国与东盟签立友好协约是发出一个强烈的信号，美国愿意深化与东盟的关系以便对付中国在东盟越来越大的影响力！"

但要如何对付中国在东盟的影响力的问题，可能要美国国务卿希拉里·克林顿大动脑筋，由于美国在金融和经济上已经面对大难题，要和中国一样，对东盟提供财经援助和开放市场是没有可能的事！

美国只能够考虑以文化产品来影响东盟，因为东南亚人民很需要，也很喜欢美国的计算机软件、电影、音乐和其他复制权利昂贵的文化产品，但大部分人都买不起，因为版权费太昂贵。

people it need but can't afford it?

America government should consider advising those production companies to reduce their copyright fee as low as possible to the ASEAN market. Because most of the ASEAN people are still living under the developing countries standard and can't afford to pay as high as those well developed countries people like Americans and Europeans.

America cultures can influence the world better than military strength. American's leaders should know how to use it.

31st, August, 2009

如果美国政府能够劝说这些产品公司，向东南亚人民只征收特别低廉的版权费，将会大受欢迎。由于东南亚人民仍生活在发展中国家，不能够和美国及欧洲用户相比。

美国文化在世界上的影响力可能比军事更强，如果美国领导人懂得如何运用它。

写于 2009 年 8 月 1 日

⊙ 美国助理国务卿克里斯托弗出席东盟与美国对话会

US should treat tourist well!

The former Hong Kong governor Christopher Patten said in his "the Obama effect" article that "American airports are as dire as British ones, maybe worse. Los Angeles gets the Oscar, with Soviet-style queues through security....and third world infrastructure......"

My personal experience in the US recently ... getting through the Los Angeles airport ...confirmed what the Patten said. Each incoming passenger will be subject to immigration official's questioning and the printing of all the fingers and camera recordings. From landing till leaving the airport took every passenger almost one hour, just to enter the world's most respected, most liberal and most efficient country.

The process of departure is also not the same as other countries in the world. Usually in most airports all the check-in luggage just goes through security check. Then handed over to the airline check-in counter and at the same time collect the boarding passes. That's all.

Whereas in the Los Angeles airport passengers go direct to the airline check-in counter to weigh the check-in luggage and obtain boarding passes then must move all the luggage personally to the security deportment for checking one by one. Regardless of whether you are the first class or economic class passengers all must wait patiently!

All international passengers from leaving the hotel till finishing the ride to the airport security spend more than three

美国应善待游客

前香港总督彭定康在他的“The Obama Effect”的文章中说："美国的机场和英国同样糟糕，可能更甚！洛杉矶机场存在着苏联式的安全检查制度和第三世界的基础设施……"

我最近到美国，也在洛杉矶机场进出境，亲自体验到令人讨厌的检查过程，应证了彭定康所说属实。每个入境旅客差不多都必须经过移民局官员的考问，以及印下所有手指模及照相存案。从下飞机到提取行李离开机场足足花了一个多小时的时间，才能带着“终于过关了”的心情踏入这个号称世界上最尊重人权、最自由、最有办事效率的国境。

离境的过程情况，和世界上其他各国也不太相同，一般机场的登机惯例是先把行李通过安全检查，然后交给航空公司称重入仓，领取登机证便完事。

但在洛杉矶机场却不相同，旅客将行李交给航空公司称重领取登机证后，必须亲自将行李再搬到安全检查部门排队等候检查，不管你是头等舱或经济舱旅客，都要耐心地等待。最重视时间的美国，在这里旅客的时间就不值钱了！

每个旅客从离开酒店搭车到机场到办完安全检查手续，再到可以登机，几乎要花上3个小时以上的时间！

美国如果要赚取更多游客的钱，就应该善待游客，给

hours of time!

If the United States wishes to earn more money from the tourist industry then she should try to treat tourists well! Offer visitors a good impression to improve the safety inspections methods and shorten the time of immigration check-in.

At the Los Angeles airport passengers were order to take off their shores for security check! It's not a scientific way of checking in a well developed scientific country!

24th, August, 2009

游客留下好印象，学习新加坡和中国，改善安全检查的方法和缩短出入境的时间。

在洛杉矶机场每个离境旅客都必须脱鞋安全检查，在一个科学大国使用这种安检方法实在太不科学了！

写于 2009 年 8 月 24 日

⊙ 美国自由女神像

The international image of the United States

At the end of the year in 2008, eight well-known global press associations conducted a survey on "the international image of the United States," and the results showed that from the beginning of the 21st century, the image world-wide of the United States has been deteriorating.

And the survey was determined by the majority of the United States allies which enjoy similar political systems, ideologies and values. 75% of French say that since Bush became president, they began to see the United States "is not pleasing to the eye". Canada, Switzerland and Japan the only United States allies in Asia, also have the above-mentioned viewpoints.

In the United States, there are more than 80% of people not very satisfied with the status of the United States. An up-to-date Georgetown University study shows that in the United States at home and abroad, the decision-making ability and competitiveness are being questioned.

After the 9.11 incident, the United States feel the need to make use of its power to change the world, but the Americans is no longer optimistic to change the world now. Because the war in Iraq and Afghanistan is too expensive! Plus the enormous military costs each year, caused the United States into an unprecedented financial and economic difficulties, it is impossible for the U.S. to change the world by force now!

What the United States should consider to do now is how to adopt a peaceful policy to improve the deteriorating international

美国国际形象

2008 年岁末，8 家著名的全球性报纸联合作了一项名为“美国国际形象”的调查，结果显示，从 21 世纪开始，世界对美国的看法一直在恶化。

在接受调查的人群中，大部分还是美国的盟友，享有与之相似的政治制度、意识形态及价值观。75% 的法国人说自从布什当上总统，他们就开始看美国“不顺眼”，加拿大、瑞士以及美国在亚洲的唯一盟友日本，持上述观点的人群分别为 77%、86% 和 62%。

在美国国内，则有超过 80% 的人对美国的现状十分不满，美国乔治城大学最新的研究显示，在美国国内外，决策能力和竞争力都在受到质疑。

911 事件之后，美国觉得要利用自己的强大来改造世界，然而现在，美国人要改造世界的乐观主义不再那么高涨了，在伊拉克和阿富汗战争所付出的代价太昂贵了！加上每年的庞大军事费用，使美国在财经上陷入了前所未有的困境，要以武力改变世界，恐怕已经心有余而力不足了！

美国现在要做的事情应该是如何以和平政策，改善恶

image! In view of this, some of my previous suggestions in my blogs could be useful for the U.S. relevant authorities to refer too.

13th, July, 2009

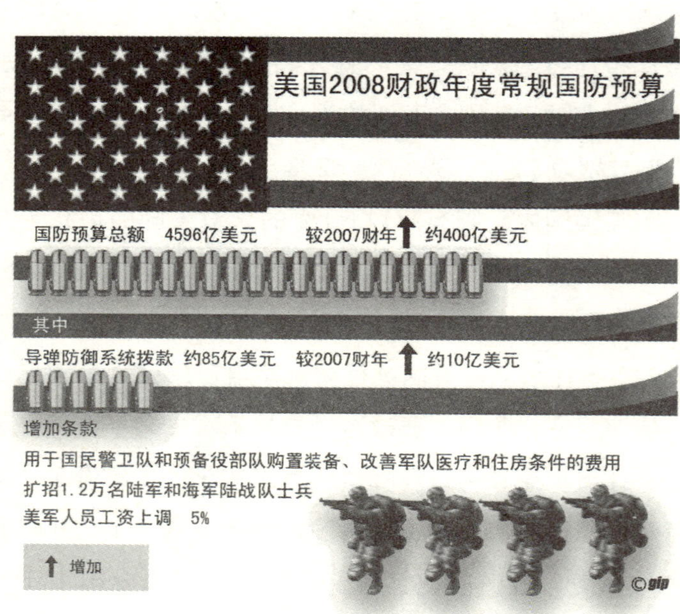

⊙ 美国众议院通过 2008 财年常规国防预算

化的国际形象。而我此前所写的博客里的一些建议，也许对此有所帮助，很值得有关当局加以参考。

写于 2009 年 7 月 13 日

⊙ 美国母亲缅怀在伊战中阵亡的儿子

Security of Embassy

10 years ago, the U.S. embassies in Kenya and Tanzania were bombed, killing 231 people including 12 Americans. The United States then actively enhanced the safety level of the overseas embassies. After 911 events in 2001 prompted Washington to start a more comprehensive security assessment plan.

U.S. State department pointed out that from now to 2013 it needs 7.5 billion US dollars to construct new buildings in about 50 locations and another 850 million US dollars for larger scale renovation in 40 locations.

But officials indicated that as a result of rising construction costs, depreciation of the US dollar, even with such a large scale of cost incurred it still not good enough to protect the security of the United States overseas delegations.

The embassy is a symbol of the sovereign rights of nation, the security concern, of course is very important. But to spend so much money to build every embassy like a fortress ....is it necessary? Is any other way to make the embassy more secure without having to spend too much money? Some suggestions below might worthwhile for the relevant authority of the United States to consider:

Those who attack the U.S. embassy may hate the United States. Therefore, first of all, the United States should consider changing all the unwelcome policies turning hostility into friendship in order to reduce the hatred toward the United States.

大使馆的安全

10 年前美国驻肯尼亚和坦桑尼亚的大使馆遭到炸弹攻击，造成包括 12 个美国人在内的 231 人丧命之后，美国就积极提升海外使馆的安全水平。2001 年的 911 事件更促使华盛顿当局展开全面的安全评估行动。

美国国务院指出：从现在到 2013 年间，它需要大约 75 亿美元在 50 个地点建造新的建筑物，以及另外 8 亿 5000 万美元在另外 40 个地点进行大规模翻新。

但是官员们指出，由于建筑成本不断上涨，美元贬值下降，这样大规模的投入还是无法保障驻海外美国使节团的安全。

大使馆是一个国家的主权象征，安全问题当然很重要，但花大量金钱把每一个大使馆建成一座坚固的防弹堡垒有必要吗？有没有其他办法可以让使馆更安全而不必花费太多的钱去建造？下面一些小建议，也许值得美国有关当局加以考虑：

攻击美国大使馆的人，一定对美国怀恨在心，所以美国应该实行“化敌为友”的政策，把仇恨美国的人数减少，以至完全根除，大使馆就不会存在不安全的问题了。

一个如此富强的美国，肯定可以变成一个世界上最令人向往、仰慕、爱戴的国家，只要领导人肯改变政策：在外交上以友善代替强权，在利益上与他国互惠，待人以博爱代替偏爱，对信仰应该求同存异，对弱小民族一视同仁，

This is the best way to solve the embassy security problems.

America is the richest and powerful country in world. It could surely be able to become one of the world's most desirable, admired, love and esteem country. As long as the leaders are willing to adopt the following policies.....On the diplomatic front must be more friendly less powerful....Sharing interest with the world equally...Love for all ...Look for common ground while reserving differences in religion....Treat the same for weak and small nations....No interference in the internal affairs of others countries...Implement the national charity for the poor without conditional....Remain neutral toward all countries and respect each other.... And do not extend the ambition to conquer the Moon and outer space. Let the people all over the world live in peace. As such, nobody would attack the U.S. embassy any more.

30th, June, 2009

对他国不干涉内政，对贫穷国家乐善好施，而且施恩不求回报，对所有国家保持中立，人不犯我，我也不犯人，不要把野心扩展到月球、火星上去，让全世界的人都能过着和平安详的日子，美国的大使馆的安全问题就可以迎刃而解了！

写于 2009 年 6 月 30 日

⊙ 美国向海地派兵加强使馆安防工作

US-Sino Joint Efforts on Hunger

The current world economy difficulties, problems with the international security and global environment problems made China and the United States understand each other better. One can see greater benefit can be achieved from cooperation. Both can rely and make use of their different strengths. These are the motivation and condition to start more cooperation of the two great countries in order to solve their own problem as well as for the whole world!"

For example, to cooperate in relief of over one billion hungry population in the world.

According to the United Nations food and agriculture group report: there are more then one billion hungry people in the world this year mainly in developing countries; the Asia-Pacific region, the largest number of hungry people about 642 million. In sub-Saharan Africa the proportion of hungry people up to 32%, the developed countries the numbers of hungry people are 15 million.

Hungry people are currently one-sixth of the world population. This situation will cause a serious risk to the world peace and security.

United Nations food and agriculture organization director general called upon to expedite the building of social security works to improve the situation.

If China and the United States in accordance with my following suggestions to join hands to relief the world of hunger... will benefit world peace and security.

中美联手救饥饿

新加坡《联合早报》言论版指出："中美联手能为世界做更多事，当前世界经济所遇到的困难，加上国际安全和全球环境等问题层出不穷，这些严峻的现实使得中美更清楚地认识了对方，从对方身上更多地看到了自己的利益，看到了可供自己借助和依赖的力量，对这两个大国来说，这是进行更多合作的条件和动力，它们自己能解决自身的问题，而且也能为整个世界成就很多事情。"

例如合作救济全球超过10亿的饥饿人口。

根据联合国粮食及农业组织报告：今年世界饥饿人口已超过10亿，主要分布在发展中国家，亚洲太平洋地区的饥饿人口数量最多，约为6.42亿，非洲撒哈拉以南地区的饥饿人口比例最高为32%，发达国家中饥饿人口数量为1500万。

目前饥饿人口占世界人口的六分之一，给世界和平安全带来严重风险。

联合国粮农组织总干事呼吁各国政府迅速建设社会保障工程，改善饥饿人口的处境。

中美两国如果能够依照下列各点建议联手救济世界饥饿人口，改善他们的处境，对世界的和平和安全以及中美两国都有好处。

美国政府已经知道只靠武力行动得不到真正的和平，每年军事费用高达数千亿美元，当世界警察也很难得到世

The U.S. government has been aware of that the use of force alone is not able to obtain a real peace environment. The military costs each year up to hundreds of billions of dollars to act as an international police but still hard to gain respect from the world!

Therefore, if the U.S. government could consider to save 10%~20% from its military expense each year to reserve 200 billion U.S. dollars as the world hungry people relief funds and get China join hand by providing cheaper than world market price of food, daily necessities etc. Both countries will surely gain a lot of good reputation from the world.

To do so, not only would one billion hungry people in the world enjoy the benefits and are grateful but people may change their unhappy attitude toward the United States. China will also benefit indirectly from the manufactures, less dependent on the U.S. market and thus reduce the pressures on American workers unemployed. It is worthwhile for the authority to consider.

22nd, June, 2009

人的好感。

因此，美国政府如果考虑把每年运用在军事行动的开销，节省 10%~20%，筹 2000 亿美元作为救济世界饥饿人口的基金，和中国联手，由中国提供比世界市价更便宜的粮食、日用品，共同解决世界饥饿人口的困难，相信将会得到世界更好的评价。

这样做，不但可以使世界 10 亿饥饿人口得到实惠而感激不尽，也将可以使对美国不满的人由于美国的善意而对美国另眼相看。中国厂家也将会间接受惠，可以减少对美国市场的依赖，进而减轻美国工人失业的压力。这是一举数得的善事、好事，很值得有关当局加以考虑。

写于 2009 年 6 月 22 日

⊙“稻米就是生命”——2004 年被定为国际稻米年

New US Envoy to China

US president Obama has nominated the governor of Utah, Jon Huntsman, a Republican as the new ambassador to China. He is a China expert speaking fluent Chinese during nomination conference at the White House. He spoke two Chinese sentences translated as: "help each other" and "learn from each other".

President Obama said he made the appointment "mindful of its extraordinary significance" and the breath of issues at stake in US-China relations, including the global economic crisis, the environment public health, human right and north Korea and Pakistan".

Jon Huntsman is a billionaire's son has major political ambitions than business. He served as ambassador to Singapore at the age of 32 the youngest ambassador of USA and he did not intend to seek for other jobs then the Utah governor. But president Obama has made him change his mind.

Jon Huntsman 49 years old has seven children of which five are his natural children and two others daughters were adopted from China and India.

China has a long history country, full of opportunities for the future with large populations. It's the economic and influence power is rising. China will be able to play an important role to challenge whatever happens in Asia and the world.

Therefore his excellence Jon Huntsman should implement the "help each other" principle and "learn from each other" spirit to help China to resolve Taiwan, Tibet and Xinjiang separatist

新任驻华大使

美国总统奥巴马提名犹他州州长，共和党人洪博培（Jon Huntsman）为新任驻华大使，他会说流利的中文，是位“中国通”。

奥巴马总统说：“中国拥有悠久的历史，充满机遇的未来，中国人口众多，经济和影响力正在提升。中国将在应对亚洲和全世界面临的重要挑战中发挥重要作用。”

洪博培是亿万富翁之子，弃商从政，原本没有打算再寻求州长之外别的职位，但奥巴马总统使他改变了他的决定。

洪博培现年 49 岁，有 7 个孩子，其中 5 个孩子是亲生子女，两个是在中国和印度所领养的女孩。他在里根总统访华时先抵北京打前站，在老布什总统手下出任过驻新加坡大使，在小布什总统第一任期内担任美国贸易副代表和贸易大使。

奥巴马的竞选经理大卫·普劳夫曾经预言洪博培有可能代表共和党参加 2012 年总统大选，在白宫提名发布会上，洪博培以中文说：“互相帮助，互相学习。”这可能是他来华任大使的抱负。但愿他的任命能顺利通过，早日上任，以便配合奥巴马总统要改变美国改变世界的宏愿，把中美关系“改变”得更好，使他“互相帮助，互相学习”的立场和精神能为中美两国的和平相处和共同利益发挥重要的作用。

problems. At the same time, China could also use their influence to help America to solve problems with North Korea, Pakistan and Iran.

Whole world people wish that America could solve the dispute with unfriendly countries peacefully. If the present and future's president of America could adopt a peace and no war policy it will certainly earn the respect and love of all people in the world. Hope President Obama and the new ambassador to China could share these ambitions.

18th, May, 2009

在“互相帮助”的原则下，协助中国解决“台独”、“藏独”、“疆独”的问题，中国亦可用其影响力协助美国解决朝鲜、巴基斯坦和伊朗等问题。

以和平政策解决世界纷争是全世界人民的愿望。现在及未来，美国总统如果能够采用爱和平不要战争的政策，一定能够得到世人的敬爱。愿奥巴马总统和新任驻华大使洪博培先生能共勉之。

写于 2009 年 5 月 18 日

⊙ 美国驻华大使洪博培夫妇携女儿杨乐意扬州寻根

US Warship Escaped From Pirate!

The spokesman of US navy fifth fleet headquartered in Bahrain disclosed that a US supply warship was run after by two Somalia pirates speedboat on May 7, 2009 in the Gulf of Aden. The supply warship was attacked by the pirates, opened fire for about one hour before escaping safely.... thanks to the limited range of the pirates' guns.

U.S. supply warship crew used the long-range acoustic warming devices to stop the pirates. What a pity incident! The U.S. navy in fact should try to speed up to catch the pirate instead of run away from them!

What happen to the world superpower's navy? Scared of Somalia pirates? Why not urge the Chinese patrol navy in the area to help! (Ha! Ha!)

Can the United Nations expect the US navy to fight Somalia pirates and safe guard the gulf of Aden with others countries navy patrol teams.

The US navy certainly is not a "paper tiger". But those people who ran away from Somalia pirates may be are!

11th, May, 2009

美舰逃离索海盗!

总部设在巴林的美国海军第五舰队发言人5月7日透露：一艘美军补给舰在亚丁湾海域遭遇两艘索马里海盗的快艇追击，并向补给舰开火，整个追逐过程长达一小时，不过因为海盗采用射程有限的武器攻击美舰，所以才没被其击中。

美舰的船员使用了远距离声学装置警告海盗快艇舰不要靠近，为了摆脱海盗的追踪，美舰最后只能加速逃离!

⊙ 安理会通过关于索马里海盗问题决议

美舰在索马里遇上海盗，没有把海盗捕捉反而加速逃离?! 这难道是世界上超强海军只能做的事吗? 为什么不向在亚丁湾巡逻的中国海军要求保护呢? 哈哈!

联合国还指望美国海军能带头把索马里海盗清除呢!

美舰肯定不是“纸老虎”，但海军官兵可能是?! 至少是那些遇海盗的人!

写于2009年5月11日

How US want the world to be?

U.S. president Obama accused China of imprisonment and harassment of journalists, during his speech to “the world press freedom day” on May 1, 2009.

Certainly it will make China unhappy. I urge America to respect and face the facts on press freedom situation in China and respect her judicial and sovereignty rights. Please put an end to “irresponsible remarks” on China. The United States' commission on international religion freedom also proposes to continue to classify China as a “country of particular concern” and condemn their religion freedom situation. Again this will upset China. The report has no factual basis and is full of prejudice. Chinese from various ethnic groups and at various locations enjoy religious worship freely by law; the facts are obvious to all.

America has repeatedly urge China to cooperate to improve the world financial and economic crisis. But on the other hand she criticizes China's press and religious freedom? Big mouth certainly will not gain!

Even thought China's press and religion policy was not as free as America. But however if every countries in the world are all adopted America freedom policy with no difference on freedom level. Then who else will still admire America freedom? American's freedom will have no value for sale!

The president of United States and smart politicians should know what kind of world could be beneficial to the US, and to

美国要怎样的世界？

美国总统奥巴马5月1日发表“世界新闻自由日”演讲时，指责中国监禁及骚扰记者，引起中国不满。中方敦促美国应该尊重事实，正确看待中国的新闻自由状况，尊重中国的司法主权，停止对中国“说三道四”。

美国国际宗教自由委员会发表2009年度报告：继续建议把中国列为“特别关注国家”，并指责中国的宗教自由状况，又引起中国的不满。中方指出美国有关的报告毫无事实依据，充满偏见，中国各民族、各地人民都依法享有宗教信仰自由，这一事实是有目共睹的。

美国口口声声要和中国合作改善世界经济和金融困境，却不忘指责中国的新闻和宗教自由状况？！肯定会言多必失！

就算中国对新闻和宗教信仰真的没有美国那样自由。但如果世界各国都和美国一样自由开放，没有程度上的差别，那还有人会向往美国的自由吗？美国的自由还有价值吗？

聪明的美国总统和政治家们应该晓得要一个什么样的

be able to attract people from not so free country to admire America's model of freedom and democracy.

11th, May, 2009

世界才对美国有利？才能使世人对美国的自由有所仰慕和向往——当然要一些和美国有所不同的国家。

写于 2009 年 5 月 11 日

⊙ 美国总统奥巴马就核峰会召开新闻发布会

America's politic and economic position will decline!

According to America's national intelligence council analysis report in the next 20 years, America political and economy dominance will decline. The U.S. dollar as the world's major currency will weaken. China with the national capitalism economic model will challenge the United States influence in wealth creation from the developed world. The wealth from the developed world began to turn to oil production nations as well as the Asian center of the manufacturing and services industries……

By 2025, although the United States will remain the world's most powerful national, but not the leadership of the world. The era is past and US could only join with other countries to play as one of the important role nations in the word.

The reasons of decline are: too ambitious to act as an international police and high expenditure on the military. Forcing the acceptance of different faiths in others countries for a free and democratic polices, created a lot of dislike for US. US print unlimited US dollars, taken too much advantage of world people. The situation of China economic is stronger and stronger. And suddenly become the U.S. nation's largest creditors. Therefore the United Stated Banknote printing machine may not be able to print any time freely in future.

In 15 years time, can the United States maintain the world's most powerful country in strength? It depends on Obama's government policy of "made more good friends, reduce old hatred" do not oppose by the congress and opposition party.

美国政经地位将衰退

美国国家情报委员会发表的分析报告说：未来 20 年美国的政治和经济支配地位将会衰退，美元作为世界主要货币地位将削弱。追随国家资本主义经济模式的中国将在多极化的世界中同美国竞争影响力。世界财富开始从发达国家转向石油出产国，以及亚洲这个制造业和服务业中心……

到 2025 年，美国虽然仍将保持全球最强大国家实力，但领导全球、叱咤风云的时代已成过去，美国只能与其他国家一道扮演世界舞台上的重要角色。

美国为什么会面临衰退呢？主要原因是：由于要担当国际警察，在军事上疯狂地消耗。以霸权手段强迫不同信仰国家接受自由民主政策造成很多世人的反感。无限量印刷美钞，在财经上占尽世人的便宜，但形势比人强，一个原来被轻蔑地称呼为“东亚病夫”的中国，却突然间变成了美国最大的债主。今后，美国的印钞机就自然不能随心所欲地开动了！

15 年后，美国是否能够保持全球最强大国家的实力，将取决于奥巴马新政府的“广交良友、减少宿敌”的政策，会不会受到国会及其政敌的阻挡。

奥巴马的外交必须走出以美国为全球中心的既有对话模式，学会尊重联合国，利用联合国，进而顺应多边主义的潮流，接受中国国家主席胡锦涛的主张：“中美关系是两

Obama foreign policy must able to get out of the exiting global center for the dialogue model and learn to respect and make use of the United Nations to conform to the trend of multilateralism and accept the idea of president Hu Jintao that "SINO-US relation are the two most important one of bilateral relations between China and the United States as the world's largest developing country and the largest developed country to human peace and development in the lofty cause of shoulder common responsibility the significance of SINO-US relations and influence for beyond the bilateral scope."

To share with China to become the two greatest countries in the world (2G) should be better to become one of the important countries in the world. Is it right? The smart U.S. leaders should know how to choose it.

28th, April, 2009

国最重要的双边关系之一，中美两国作为世界上最大的发展中国家和最大的发达国家，对人类和平与发展的崇高事业肩负共同责任，中美关系的意义和影响远远超出双边范畴。”

和中国分享世界二强（2G）好过“只能与其他国家一道扮演世界舞台上的重要角色之一”。聪明的美国领导人应该懂得如何选择。

写于 2009 年 4 月 28 日

⊙ 中国评级机构首发国家信用报告

The US wants to help Myanmar

The United States deputy secretary of state Steinberg said: “we are looking forward to work with ASEAN countries, China, India and Japan to discuss a common strategy in order to help Myanmar to improve their people’s living standard as well as for policy to the stability of this region”.

Myanmar is one of 10 member countries of ASEAN with a population of about 47million and most of the people are Buddhists. In recent decades the country is run by the military dictatorship. Resulting in slow development, economic backwardness as well as the hardship on people’s lives!

Some Asian countries tried to persuade the country of Myanmar to change policies. The United States and the European Union impose sanctions and put pressures on the government of Myanmar to release democratic leader Aung San Suu Kyi… but all are not effective.

If the United States is to continue to force a high-handed approach to improve the human rights situation in Myanmar the release of the democracy leader Aung San Suu Kyi! Certainly will not succeed!

If the America really wants to change the political situation of Myanmar then it should look for solution from the military is “whoever started the trouble should end it!” therefore one must adopt a friendly attitude toward the military government. And urge the assistance of the Chinese government to convey the following recommendations to the government of the Myanmar in

美国要协助缅甸？

美国常务副国务卿斯坦伯格说：“我们希望与亚细安国家、中国、印度和日本讨论共同策略以便找出有助于改善缅甸人民生活，以及促进此一关键地区的稳定政策。”

缅甸是亚细安10个成员国之一，人口约4700多万，大部分人民信仰佛教，近几十年来都由军人专权执政，以致发展迟慢，经济落后，人民生活困苦！

一些亚洲国家虽曾尝试劝缅甸改变治国政策，美国和欧盟甚至实施制裁，对缅甸政府施加压力，要它释放民主领袖翁山淑支，但都没有效果。

原因是：缅甸为鱼米之乡，天然资源丰富，人民生活简单，大部分信奉佛教，反抗性不强，只要生活能过得去，军人执政，习惯已成自然！政治上民主与否，似乎问题不大。因此美国如果继续要以高压手段迫使缅甸改善人权状况和释放民主领袖翁山淑支，这肯定不会成功！

美国要改变缅甸的政治状况，也许只有对执政的军人下工夫，所谓解铃还须系铃人！以友善态度对待军政府，通过中国政府的协助，试采用下列几点建议，以换取缅甸政府实行“更开放、尊重人民的权利，以及融入环球经济的政策”。

1. 美国国会议员应该停止对缅甸最高领导人的指责，因为军人只会吃软不吃硬的。

2. 欢迎缅甸军政府领导人和军官们以贵宾身份访问美

exchange for a "more open and respect of human rights as well as the policy of integration into global economy". Such as:

1. Members of the U.S. Congress should stop accusing top leaders of Myanmar.

2. Welcome the Myanmar military leaders and military official to visit the United States as a VIP. And privately to ensure that their future position and interested in exchange for their China's type of "open-door policy".

3. Promise to provide military assistance to Myanmar in exchange for the core objective of the United States.

4. Open up U.S. market for the Myanmar's products with preference terms of import duty in order to encourage Myanmar to implement China-type of "Free market economy" policy.

Should the U.S. government able to implement the above suggestions the leaders of the military government may be more enthusiastic to democratic policy and more respect human rights than Aung San Suu Kyi in time to come.

7th, April, 2009

国，私下保证他们的前途和利益，以换取他们实行中国式的“开放政策”。

3. 许诺对缅甸提供军事援助，以换取美国的核心目标。

4. 开放美国市场给缅甸产品优惠进口以鼓励缅甸实行中国式的“自由经济市场”政策。

美国政府如果能够实行上述各点，假以时日，缅甸军政府的领导人也许将会比翁山淑支更懂民主、更尊重人权！

写于 2009 年 4 月 7 日

⊙ 盖茨表示阿富汗战争失败后果严重

Good News for Americans

Good News for Americans! In February 2009, when the U.S. President B. Obama decided to increase U.S. troops in Afghanistan I gave my immediate feedback in my blog that "increase troops not a resolution". One month after we are pleased to see the below newspaper headline "Obama seeks way out of Afghanistan". This is the good news for Americans! "What we're looking for is comprehensive strategy. There's got to be an exit strategy". Mr. Obama said in a wide-ranging interview shown on Sunday in the U.S. as the attached report. If his plan is not going to vote down by the congress Americans may be able to avoid another miserable war like Iraq.

Here are some of the comprehensive exit strategy for President Obama to consider: Using part of the military saving money to subsidize the followings:

1. Offer to sell America's made car to Afghanistan at 50% of concession price for a period of 5 years (to upgrade their living standard and helping American car industry. one stone two birds)

2. Allow all Afghanistan to use computer software, movie, and music without paying royal fee and copy rights (culture influence is worthwhile

3. Build Low Cost Housing for sale to Afghanistan at a discount price. (People will always appreciate).

4. Build more schools and hospitals for the whole country.

美国人的好消息

今年 2 月当美国奥巴马总统宣布要增兵阿富汗时，我马上在我的博客上指出“增兵不是办法”，只过一个月的时间，我们很高兴地看到下列剪报的大标题“奥巴马要从阿富汗撤退”，这真是美国人的好消息！奥巴马总统在接受媒体访问时说：“我们在寻求撤出阿富汗的良策，相信将会找出适当的办法。”如果他的计划不会被国会否决的话，美国将可能避免另一场“伊拉克式的悲惨战争”。

这里有一些撤出后的良策可供奥巴马总统参考，利用部分停战省下来的军事费用赞助下列各方面所需要的开销：

1. 将美国制造的汽车以 50% 折扣的优惠价卖给阿富汗人，为期 5 年（一方面可以提高阿富汗人的生活水平，也可协助美国汽车寻求市场，是一石二鸟的善策）。

2. 让所有阿富汗人不必缴纳美国电脑软件、电影和音乐的知识版权费（文化影响的价值可收回代价）。

3. 建造大量廉价屋，以低价卖给阿富汗人（人们将会永远感激美国的好处）。

4. 为阿富汗各地方建造大量学校和医院（受良好教育水准及身体健康的人民就不想要当恐怖分子了）。

(More well educated and healthy people fewer become terrorism).

5. Learning from China as how to maintain good relationship with most of Muslim countries.

31st, March, 2009

5. 向中国学习怎么样才能够和伊斯兰国家建立良好的关系?

写于 2009 年 3 月 31 日

⊙ 美阿军队统一销毁在阿富汗境内收缴的军火

Make Use of the World Expo!

Since 1992 the U.S. Congress has prohibited the use of State fund to take part in the World Expo! Therefore, the world super country had no choice but to withdraw from the 2000 World Expo in Hanoverian of Germany due to lack of funding. The 2005 World Expo in Japan was financed with the assistance of Japanese companies for the America's exhibition hall!

The 2010 Shanghai world expo is scheduled for opening in May next year. Yet the construction funds for the America's exhibition hall are still nowhere to be found! It is hard to believe! The Leaders of America once said: The United States needs the world and the world needs the United States! And why must the United States Congress give up the world stage?

American leaders also have said: China and the United States should cooperate to improve the world economy. As such then they should make good use of the business gathered in the Shanghai world expo. The United States can take the advantage of this opportunity to offer the U.S. best quality and good prices of properties for sale, to present the U.S. Universities to recruit oversea students, showing the most attractive tourist spots to attract the world tourist, showing the world most popular movies, music and promote various high-tech products, and bring-in the most prestigious sports events like NBA basketball entertain and capture for the broad masses of the China and world markets. There will certainly be an unexpected good harvest.

The new leaders of the Unites States should consider

利用世博会

美国国会从 1992 年起就禁止美国国务院动用国家财政参展世博会，以致这个世界超级强国于 2000 年因为资金不足而退出在德国汉诺威举办的世博会。而 2005 年日本爱知世博会是在日本企业的协助下才完成国家馆的建设的。

2010 年上海世博会明年 5 月便开幕了！然而美国馆的建设资金还没有着落，真令人难以相信，美国领导人曾经说过：美国需要世界，世界也需要美国。而美国国会却要把这个世界舞台放弃？

美国领导人也曾经说过：中国和美国应该合作把世界经济搞好，那就应该好好利用这个万商云集的上海世博会，作为两国合作的出发点：美国可以利用这个机会通过和中方合作，把美国价廉物美的房地产业，各大学要招收的学生额，最能吸引旅客的旅游点，最受世界欢迎的电影、音乐，以及各种高科技产品及最负盛名的运动项目，如篮球表演等介绍给世人。争取广大的中国和世界市场，肯定会有意想不到的收获。

changing the policy on the Expo and asking Congress to use the State fund to finance the participation in the World Expo.

10th, March, 2009

美国新领导人应该改变轻视世博会的政策，敢于要求国会变不准动用国家财政参与世博会的决定。

写于 2009 年 3 月 10 日

⊙ 美国国务卿主持仪式庆祝上海世博会美国馆开馆

Improving US Budget Deficit

China plans to increase its 2009 defense budget by 14.9% percent to RMB 480.6 billion equivalent to US$ about 70 billion. Most western media and a Singapore Chinese newspaper widely reported that China is expanding its military forces aggressively.

This is despite what China said that the defense expenditure was fairly low compared with other countries considering the size of China population and territory. The United States defense budget for the fiscal year 2009 is US$515 billion that does not include for Iraq and Afghanistan and some spending on nuclear weapon. No western media is interested to report this.

China is a country with 1.3 billion populations having annual military budget only about 70 billion. Whereas America with only 312 million of population, but the annual military budget as high as 515 billion. From this one can see very clearly that who got the wild ambition in military? For this we can see that the western newspapers are not balanced in their reporting.

More confusing was Pentagon reported that China's actual military cost are three times the published data,...their total spending for last year was 97-139 billion U.S. dollar. Even if true but compare to the 515 billion of United State budget it's still much less. The authority concerned should immediately reduce their spending. Otherwise it would be difficult to improve their budget deficit.

9th, March, 2009

改善美国赤字

中国公布2009年国防预算为人民币4806亿元，约等于700亿美元，增长率为14.9%，西方报纸就纷纷加以报道，包括新加坡《联合早报》！字里行间，觉得中国有扩充军力的企图。

当中国指出所提高的军事费用，如果以国家人口和土地面积和其他国家比较是合理和适度的，美国2009年的国防预算总额为5150亿美元，还不包括用于伊拉克、阿富汗和核化设备的费用，却似乎没有一家西方报纸加以提及！

一个13亿人口的中国，每年的军事开销只约700亿美元，而一个只有3亿人口的美国，每年的军事开销却高值5150亿美元，谁有军事野心？聪明的西方记者却装糊涂对此一句话不说？！

⊙ 刘建超表示美指责中方“军费开支不透明”毫无道理

更糊涂的还是美国五角大楼，竟指出中国的实际军事费用是公布数据的三倍，评估中国去年的军费总额是在970亿美元至1390亿美元之间，就算是事实，但比美国每年的5150亿美元仍少得很多！相比之下，无异是在告诉其人民，美国每年的军费开销实在是太多了！有关当局应该赶快节流，否则国家的赤字将难以改善！

写于2009年3月9日

In Words and Deeds

The US president Barack Obama told the Congress on his speech regarding his foreign policy that: "... in words and deeds we are showing the world that a new era of engagement has begun for we know the America cannot meet the threats of this century alone. ... We cannot shun the negotiating table nor ignore the foes and forces that could do us harm"

This is the good news for the peace-loving people of the whole world, but one still have to wait and see for the real actions?

Recently, the assistant secretary of state for Asia and Pacific affairs Christopher state that the secretary of state Hillary Clinton had expressed to the China leaders during her visits: The United States is looking forward to see the progress on cross-strait negotiations on Taiwan's international activity space? To this one can see that America has not changed in her policy of protecting Taiwan!

If America really wants to abandon the "hegemony" stand, she first should abolish the "Taiwan Relation Act" and to refrain from selling weapons to Taiwan. This is the right move to help Taiwan to get their international space without any United States protection. Taiwan will then have to talk to the mainland China under the principle of one country two systems for peaceful resolution. Then Taiwan like Hong Kong will be able to entitle to abroad international relationship activity.

If the United States truly wants to put diplomatic force ahead

言论与行动

美国总统奥巴马首次向国会发表演讲时正式为其新政府的外交政策定调。他说："美国与世界接合的新时代已经到来。美国政府将与其他国家合作应对共同面临的挑战，美国无法对谈判桌视而不见，奥巴马政府将把外交置于武力之上，以'文斗'取代传统'武斗'。"

这是全世界热爱和平的人喜欢听到的话和喜欢看到的事实，但人们还要"听其言，看其行"？

近日，美国国务院主管亚太事务助理国务卿希尔指出："国务卿希拉里·克林顿访问中国时曾向中国大陆领导人表达，美国期盼两岸对扩大台湾国际空间的谈判继续取得进展。"美国关心台湾的国际空间，这说明对"保护"台湾的立场仍没有改变！

美国如果真的要放弃"霸权主义"，那就应该取消《与台湾关系法》和宣布不再售卖武器给台湾，这才是要使台湾拥有国际空间的正确做法。台湾如果没有美国的"非法保护"，就会和大陆在"一国两制"的原则下和平相处，和香港一样享有广阔的国际空间。

美国如果真要把外交置于武力之上，以"文斗"代替"武斗"，就应该把驻日本的军事基地搬走，不要让日本在日美安保条约下有恃无恐，非法占据中国的钓鱼岛，让中国和日本以"文斗"方式谈判解决钓鱼岛问题。

"military might". She should also consider moving out the military base in Japan and do not let Japan make use of the Japan-US security treaty without fear: to illegally occupy China's Diaoyu Island. So China and Japan can negotiate settlement of the Diaoyu Island issue peacefully.

However, if the United States continue to maintain Taiwan's relations act and continue to sell weapons to Taiwan and continue to base its military in Japan threatening China's security. That will prove that the new president "in words and deeds" does not match. Why does the new government still continue its policy of spending foolish and thankless money to the world affairs!

Time has change! Situation is difference! The United States should consider a new alliance with China in order to gain the greatest benefits in Asia.

2nd, March, 2009

相反地：如果美国继续保留《与台湾关系法》，继续售卖武器给台湾，继续在日本驻军威胁中国的安全。那就证明美国新政府言行不符，要继续在世界各地花钱做吃力不讨好的傻事！

势易时移，美国要在亚洲取得最大的利益应该联合中国才对。

写于2009年3月2日

⊙外交部发言人表示中国坚决反对美国对台军售

Surge is not the answer!

America President Barack Obama had decided to send more troops to Afghanistan because he believed that the hotbeds of 9.11 events, were in Afghanistan not in Iraq. But the Bush administration's focus was Iraq as the main battlefield to counter terrorism and that's why the terrorism was growing continually. Thus Obama think America should continue to fight in Afghanistan against Osama Bin Laden and his Al-Qaeda in order eliminate the culprit of 9.11 terrorist's acts and to solve the U.S. homeland security threats.

But Only 34% of Americans supported the surge plan according to an opinion poll by Washington Post and there are 44% Afghans thought that foreign troops in Afghanistan should be reduced according to a BBC report. The Afghan people were also dissatisfied with foreign troops because there were a lot of civilian casualties. In these circumstances, it is really hard for America to win the fighting in Afghanistan even with more troops there!

Fortunately, President Obama stressed that the U.S. military cannot solve the Afghan problem and cannot be used to pre-surge strategy in Afghanistan.. Only the integrated use of military, political, economic and diplomatic means multi-pronged approach can win the fighting in Afghanistan.

The United States has spent hundreds of billions of dollars, at the expense of thousands of lives to eradicate Saddam. If, fighting in Afghanistan continues, America may have to pay the same price like the Iraq in order to capture or kill Osama bin

增兵不是办法!

美国总统奥巴马决定增兵阿富汗，因为他认为布什政府将伊拉克作为反恐重心，忽略了911事件的策源地，而真正的反恐主战场是阿富汗，这是布什政府“越反越恐”的关键所在。美国应把打击和消灭911事件的罪魁祸首乌萨马·本·拉登和他的基地组织作为主要反恐任务，以便解决对美国本土安全的威胁。

但《华盛顿邮报》所做的民意调查显示，只有34%的美国人支持增兵计划。据美国和英国的广播公司的民调，44%的阿富汗人认为应当减少外国驻军，只有18%的人同意外国增兵。联合国和阿富汗政府都指出，阿富汗民众对外国驻军不满，因为战争造成不少平民伤亡。在这种情况下，美国增兵阿富汗的计划成功概率不高，难以达到目的。

幸好，奥巴马总统强调“不能用增兵来预设美军未来在阿富汗的战略基地”，他指出“光靠军事手段不能解决阿富汗问题，只有综合运用军事、政治、经济和外交等手段，多管齐下，美国才能在阿富汗及周边取得明确和可实现的目标”。

美国在伊拉克花了几千亿美元，牺牲了几千条性命才消灭了萨达姆，在阿富汗如再打下去，可能要付出同样的代价才能达到目的。但就算把乌萨马·本·拉登活捉或打死，铲除他的基地组织，全世界9亿伊斯兰人中难免仍有

Laden and the eradication of Al-Qaeda. But there are 900 million of Muslims in the world, some of them may want to revenge for Osama Bin Laden-thus American security is still threatened. So surge is not the answer!

Therefore, in order to avoid a repeat of 9.11 tragedy, the United States consider to "return evil for good", think of a best way to reconcile with the Muslim world. President Obama may have to make a major change to take a big initial step like pardoning the criminals of the 9.11 attack. This will demonstrate that the U.S.does not want to be the enemy of Muslim forever, as Chinese proverb said: "problems with the "enemy should be resolved but not make worse." US should try to ask China for help persuade all Muslims to give up their resentments toward Americans and to be friendly to each other for the peace of the world.

23rd, February, 2009

存心要为乌萨马·本·拉登报仇的人，对美国安全的威胁，仍旧不能完全解除！

因此，为避免911事件的重演，美国应该以和为贵，想办法与伊斯兰国家取得和解。奥巴马总统也许应该在政策上做一个重大的改变，主动跨出第一步：宣布对911肇事者给予宽恕，以行动证明美国不是伊斯兰的敌人。中国谚语说："冤家宜解不宜结。"同时，利用中国对伊斯兰国家的良好关系协助劝说，为世界和平放弃一切恩怨，求同存异，友好相处。

写于2009年2月23日

⊙ 美国著名妇女反战组织成员到参议院听证会现场抗议

Don't spoil your trip!

The U.S. State Secretary Mrs. Hillary Clinton said before her departure to visit Asia (including China) "The positive co-operation between U.S. and China is very important for the benefit of both countries, as well as important to the peace, progress and prosperous of Asia-Pacific Region and even the world."

But on the other hand, she gave answer to the reporter that "The U.S. government will continue to sell defensive arms to Taiwan" according to the Taiwan relations act.

Her straight- forward speaking could be habits of most Americans leader. But since she wanted to exercise her "smart power" policy, then she should avoid saying something that could embarrass the Chinese counterpart at such important moment!

One must understand how to give face to one's host especially when you need help or co-operation.

20th, February, 2009

不要影响亚洲之行

美国国务卿希拉里·克林顿起程访问亚洲四国（包括中国）之前，在亚洲协会纽约总部发表演讲时说："美国将继续致力于与中国发展积极的合作关系；两国将从对方的成功中受益；同时有助于对方的发展。这对亚太地区乃至全球和平进步与繁荣至关重要。"

但在旅途中回答记者询问时说，"根据《与台湾关系法》，美国仍将继续销售防卫性武器给台湾。"这可能是大部分美国领导人说话爽直的习惯。

但希拉里国务卿既然要实行"理性"的外交政策，就不应该在如此重要的时刻说出可能使中国领导人不乐意听的话。

聪明的政治家应该懂得给主人讲些乐意听的话，尤其当你希望得到人家的帮助和合作的时刻。否则可能造成事倍功半的结果，影响亚洲之行！

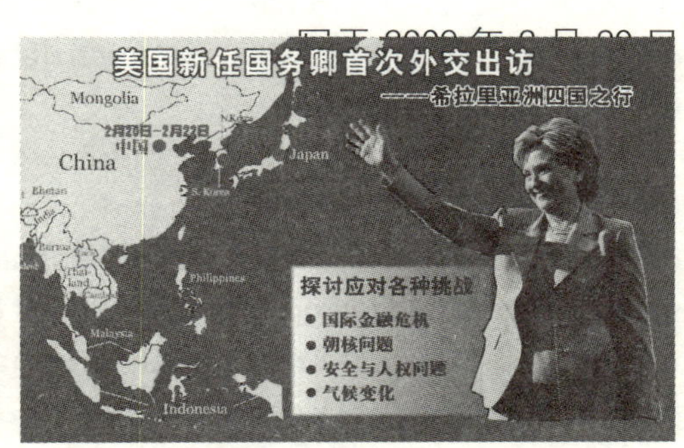

⊙ 美国新任国务卿希拉里出访亚洲四国

The Sensible Defense Secretary

The new president of United State, President Obama's decision to retain Defense Secretary Robert Gates of Bush administration was surprising to many outsiders since Obama's new policy is against Iraq War. Why was the man responsible for the Iraq War retained?

However, we may now understand the reasons after reading the frank and sensible statement by Robert Gates as follows:

"The United States defense secretary Robert Gates recently remarked that when saddled with the financial crisis, the Iraq war and war in Afghanistan, the arms procurement model needs to be revolutionized to reduce costs. He clearly stated that at present, the biggest military challenge to the United States comes from the war in Afghanistan.

Gates was attending the hearing of the senate armed services committee and this is the first time he openly expounded on US military strategy since retaining his position as Defense Secretary. According to him, the US military cannot "purchase everything" at this stage with the deteriorated economy and the enormous cost of two wars.

Gates acknowledged that there are many problems in the existing procurement model. For example, the lack of procurement experts, the incessant dispute among interested parties and the budgetary instability led to "a number of expensive weapons procurement projects" that have "unacceptable problems" in terms of cost and research and development. In

理智的国防部长

美国新总统奥巴马让布什政府的末任国防部长盖茨留任，使很多外人觉得奇怪，奥巴马总统是反对伊拉克战争的，为什么要让负责伊拉克战争的国防部长留任呢？

直到最近读了盖茨国防部长下列的谈话，才知道奥巴马要把盖茨留任的原因：

美国国防部长罗伯特·盖茨近日说：受到金融危机、伊拉克战争和阿富汗战争拖累，武器采购模式亟待革新，以节省开支。他明确提出，现阶段，美国最大的军事挑战来自阿富汗战争。

盖茨当天在参议院军事委员会出席听证会，这是他留任以来首次公开阐述美方军事战略。按照他的说法，现阶段，经济形势恶化，两场战争耗费巨大，美军不能随心所欲地“采购一切”。

盖茨承认，现有采购模式存在诸多问题，如缺乏采购专家、各方面利益争执不断、预算不稳定，导致“一些昂贵的武器采购项目”在成本、研发等方面出现“令人无法接受的问题”。在他看来，美军各兵种联合作战能力日益提高，但装备采购“各自为战”，出现重复、浪费。

他的主张符合奥巴马总统要改变美国政策的立场，节省军事开销，拼好国内金融经济是美国正确的新政策。

his view, the US joint combat capability of the various arms has progressively improved. However, the equipment procurement projects are "fragmented wars" and appear duplicated and wasteful.

His position is in line with President Obama's revised policy. Cutting military spending and fixing US domestic finance and economy are appropriate policies of United States.

The United States' defense budget is the highest in the world. In 2007 military spending was 546.8 billion US dollars, accounting for more than 40 percent of global military spending. This could be the reason most American are in debt! In fact, if the United States only takes care of its national defense and does not worry about other countries' security, all Americans could still be living a comfortable and safe life.

6th, February, 2009

美国国防预算高居世界首位，2007 年军费开支 5468 亿美元，占全球军费开支 40% 以上，这可能就是造成大多数美国人负债的原因之一，美国如果只管好自己的国防，不要担心他国的安全，所有美国人，将可以安全地过着舒适的生活。

写于 2009 年 2 月 6 日

⊙ 美国国防部长罗伯特·盖茨回答记者提问

How to be a "smart power"

If the US state secretary Mrs. Hillary "smart power" policy is meant to retain US as a super power country, US must be smart enough. In view of this, I would like to suggest the followings "Smart" policies for the US leaders to consider:

1. Do not interfere with other countries internal affairs in order to avoid too many people being unhappy with America.

2. Use United Nations or join hand with leading country in difference territory to solve the regional issues instead of doing it alone.

For example in Asia, China could help US to solve problems with North Korea, Pakistan and Afghanistan as well as all the Muslim countries because her good relationship with these countries.

The experience of China to handle the more than 30 millions of internal Muslims to live with non-Muslim peacefully could help America improve relationship with Muslim countries. In return America should help China to solve the Taiwan problems.

3rd, February, 2009

如何做聪明的强国

如果美国新政府要以“聪明手段”（“smart power”）继续成为超强国家，那下列几点建议也许值得美国领导人参考：

1. 不要干涉别国的内政，以免太多人不喜欢美国。

2. 利用联合国和个别地区的领导国家合作，共同解决每个地区的难题，代替单边主义政策。

在亚洲，只有中国才是美国的最好合作伙伴，因为中国和朝鲜、巴基斯坦、阿富汗及所有伊斯兰教国家都有很好的关系。

中国能使国内超过 3 千多万的回族人民和其他民族和平相处，足以证明中国有能力可以使其他伊斯兰教国家和美国改善关系。

写于 2009 年 2 月 3 日

The Strange Buyers

Normally, people would prefer to buy products with cheaper price and better quality goods. Sometimes buyers even try to bargain very hard in order to get the best price possible.

However, America often criticized that China has sold goods at low prices in the U.S. market using subsidy policy. This has resulted in unemployment and trade imbalance between the two countries. In view of this American government frequently complain to WTO and threaten to levy heavier import duty on some goods imported from China. America is a real strange buyer in the world indeed!

The reason American consumer goods cannot compete with China imported products is because America people living standard is much higher leading to high costs of production. It is not because China intentionally lowers the prices of their Chinese products.

Regarding the high rate of U.S. unemployment I think it is because America is well developed country. She uses high technology and automated equipment for production. As such workers are replaced by machines. As long as America does not sell high-tech manufacturing equipment to China, the trade with China will continue to deficit.

If the United States is determined to impose heavy imported duty on China goods she not only will breach the WTO treaty but also lead to rising cost of living for Americans. The general public life will turn from bad to worse. It should try to develop good

奇怪买家

一个正常的人，买东西的时候肯定会选择物美价廉的产品，有时为了捡便宜，还要与物主大力杀价、斤斤计较，以达到折扣优惠的目的。

但美国政府，对物美价廉的中国进口货却不断指责，认为中国是采用津贴及减税出口政策，才能够把大量货物以低廉的价格出口卖到美国，影响其国产货的市场，造成工人失业，形成中美贸易不平衡。

美国是世界上少有的奇怪买家，有便宜的货不买，反而埋怨中国货卖得太便宜！还对中国提出警告，如果不改变这种贸易政策，美国政府将向世贸投诉，并要对中国货物征收繁重进口税。

美国货不敌中国货，是因为美国人民生活水平高，生产成本也跟着昂贵，中国是发展中国家，工资低廉，所以能够生产物美价廉的产品，这是很自然的趋势。

美国失业率高，是因为高科技化和自动化生产的结果，不是中国的便宜货所造成的，对中国贸易入超是因为美国自私和怕输，不肯将高科技产品卖给中国的原因。

如果美国决意对中国进口货征收繁重进口税，不但违背了世贸协约，也将会提高人民的生活费用，使一般平民的生活雪上加霜，抵制中国货进口也将会影响中美的友好

Sino-US friendly relationship to bring benefits to the America. U.S. government must think twice before taking action to impose heavy import duties on China goods.

31st, December, 2008

关系，对美国是有害无利的，聪明的美国领导人应该三思而后行之。

写于 2008 年 12 月 31 日

⊙ 美对华油井管反倾销初裁带歧视性的漫画

Rescind Taiwan Relation Act

I wonder how many Americans including President-elect Obama have ever read the "Taiwan Relations Act". For the easy reference and comment on this exiting act by the public. I therefore print it out herewith for Americans especially for the President to consider rescinding this 30 year-old useless act, in order to secure the better and larger benefit with China. This should be one of the U.S. policies that he wanted to change.

The Taiwan Relations Act is an act of the United States Congress passed in 1979 after the establishment of relations with the People's Republic of China (PRC) and the breaking of relations between the United States and the Republic of China (ROC) on the island of Taiwan by President Jimmy Carter. It more clearly defines the American position on Taiwan and its cross-strait relationship with Beijing.

The act authorizes quasi-diplomatic relations with the ROC government by giving special powers to the American Institute in Taiwan to the level that it is the de facto embassy, and states that any international obligations previously made between the ROC and U.S. before 1979 are still valid unless otherwise terminated. One agreement that was unilaterally terminated by President Carter upon the establishment of relations was the Sino-American Mutual Defense Treaty; that termination was the subject of the Supreme Court case Goldwater v. Carter.

The act provides for Taiwan to be treated under U.S. laws the same as "foreign countries, nations, states, governments, or

废除《与台湾关系法》

我不知道有几个美国人，包括奥巴马总统，曾经读过这个《与台湾关系法》条文？为了让人们容易了解这个《与台湾关系法》的存在，我决意将其翻译原文印给大家参阅。特别是奥巴马总统，借此让他考虑是否应该将这个存在 30 年之久，已经没有作用的法律废除，以便和中国换取更好更多的利益，实现他要改变美国政策的意愿：

《与台湾关系法》（英语：Taiwan Relations Act；缩写：TRA）是一部现行的美国国内法。1979 年，美国与在台湾的“中华民国”政府断交而与中华人民共和国政府建交后，美国国会制定此法并由美国总统签署生效，以规范往后的美台关系。因应美台双方交流无法以“国际条约”为之，而以美国国内法形式制订，规范美国政府（对国际无效力），其目的在于取代遭废除的《中美共同防御条约》（Sino-American Mutual Defense Treaty）。

《与台湾关系法》于 1979 年 4 月 10 日经美国总统吉米·卡特签署生效。美国订定《与台湾关系法》的要旨为：“我们支持一个中国政策，但统一如何以和平方式达成要靠双方进行两岸对话。如果中共企图以武力而非对话来达成，美国将提供军事物资使它无法成功。”该法规定，如果中国试图通过武力统一台湾，将是对“西太平洋地区和平与稳定的重大威胁”。

另一方面，根据该法，美国得以在台湾设立美国在台

similar entities". The act provides that for most practical purposes of the U.S. government, the absence of diplomatic relations and recognition will have no effect.

The act defines the term "Taiwan" includes, as the context may require, the islands of Taiwan (the main Island) and Penghu, which form the Taiwan Province of the Republic of China. The act does not apply to Jinmen or Matsu.

The act stipulates that the United States will "consider any effort to determine the future of Taiwan by other than peaceful means, including by boycotts or embargoes, a threat to the peace and security of the Western Pacific area and of grave concern to the United States" but does not mandate that the United States intervene in these situations.

This act also requires the United States "to provide Taiwan with arms of a defensive character", and "to maintain the capacity of the United States to resist any resort to force or other forms of coercion that would jeopardize the security, or the social or economic system, of the people on Taiwan." Successive U.S. administrations have sold arms to the ROC in compliance with the Taiwan Relations Act despite demands from the PRC that the U.S. following legally non-binding Three Joint Communiqués and the U.S. government's proclaimed One-China policy (which differs from the PRC's One-China Policy). The Taiwan Relations Act does not require the U.S. to intervene militarily if the PRC attacks or invades Taiwan, and the U.S. has adopted a policy of "strategic ambiguity" in which the U.S. neither confirms nor denies that it would intervene in such a scenario.

The PRC does not recognize the legitimacy of the Taiwan Relations Act as it is viewed by them as "an unwarranted intrusion by the United States into the internal affairs of China." The Three

协会。值得注意的是，该法15条延续了《中美共同防御条约》的宗旨，“台湾”一词仅包括台湾及澎湖列岛，而不包含“中华民国”实际治理的金门、乌坵、马祖、东引、东沙、南沙群岛。

《与台湾关系法》亦未表示美国对台湾主权现状的认定以及未来归属的看法，只是一个规范美国政府对华政策的法律。美国政府宣称，美国政府官方对于台湾问题的立场是基于“中美三个联合公报和《与台湾关系法》”。但是，中华人民共和国政府方面始终认为该法干涉中国内政，而反对该法，并坚持游说美国参议院、众议院修改或废除该法。“中华民国”方面则不十分满意该法对于台美双方之关系规范不够明确，因而曾一度推动美国国会订立更为明确的《台湾安全加强法》以取代《与台湾关系法》，但此案最后无疾而终。

《与台湾关系法》具有三个主要功能：一、记载美国对台湾政策的目标，包括维持台海和平稳定，维持台海现状，维持美台商业及文化关系、保障人权与台湾安全。法律中明确指出任何企图以非和平方式（包括杯葛或禁运）解决台湾未来的作为，均会威胁太平洋和平与安全，美国将严重关切；美国将继续提供防卫性武器给台湾；美国也将抵抗任何诉诸武力，或使用其他高压手段，危及台湾人民安全与社会经济制度的行动。但并未表示，一旦台海发生战乱，美军有义务出兵护台，亦未明确表示，如果台海危机是由台湾方面挑起，美方应具体如何回应。二、在无外交关系的情况下，维持台美间经贸关系。将台湾比照其他主权国家办理。三、授权成立美国在台协会（American Institute in Taiwan；AIT）以代表新关系中的美方。

Joint Communiqués were signed in 1972, 1979, and 1982. The United States declared that "the United States would not formally recognize Chinese sovereignty over Taiwan" as part of the Six Assurances offered to Taipei in 1982. In the late 1990s, the United States Congress passed a non-binding resolution stating that relations between Taiwan and the United States will be honored through the TRA first. This resolution, which puts greater weight on the TRA's value over that of the three communiqués, was signed by President Bill Clinton as well.

After reading America's self-imposed Taiwan Relations Act I wonder if Americans feel like the Chinese bearing this unreasonable act forever. 30 years pass by situation have changed and the China is no longer an old country. Taiwan is safe now and also closer to the mainland China. It's time for the clever American leaders to hand over the Taiwan to China with the conditions instead of let it go free later.

22nc, December, 2008

读了这个美国单方面成立的法律，假定你是中国人，你会有何感想？中国领导人，会永远忍气吞声吗？如果迫于形势非对台湾动武不可，美国能够承担得起保护台湾的责任吗？经过 30 年的改变，中国实际上已经再不是原本的国家了，台湾不但安全和大陆也更接近了，聪明的美国领导人，到了应该考虑把台湾有条件归还中国的时候了，以免日后一无所得！

写于 2008 年 12 月 22 日

⊙ 美高官回应马英九“永不说”：乐见两岸关系和平发展

Lucky President Bush

14 December 2008 America President Bush was on a secret visit to Iraq to bid farewell.

During a press conference an Iraqi reporter among the audience suddenly threw a pair of his shoes at him 6 meters away.

Luckily shoes and not something else. The accident just scared him. He was not hurt but this could be a good warning for the new president to consider his new policy on the following:

1. Reduce the Muslim hatred for Americans

2. Change military policy. A powerful military action may change a country's political power but cannot change the thinking of its people.

3. Increase America's military power in Afghanistan is another worthless war!

19th, December, 2008

布什好运！

12 月 14 日，美国总统布什秘密告别访问伊拉克时，在记者招待会上被一个伊拉克电视台记者扔了一双鞋子。

当时这名记者距离布什只有 6 米左右，如果他扔的不是鞋子，那布什总统的生命便不堪设想了！

可幸这场意外只是有惊无险，但新的美国总统也许会得到下列几点启示：

1. 如何减少穆斯林对美国人的仇恨？

2. 强大的军事行动，可能会改变一个国家的政权，但改变不了其人民的思想。

3. 增兵阿富汗可能又是一场得不偿失的战争！

写于 2008 年 12 月 19 日

⊙ 布什卸任仍遭美国民众戏弄

Americans should pay attention...

20~30 years later, your child may have to serve coffee to the Chinese boss?

Hong Kong (Asia Times Online) pointed out that the U.S. defense budget is six times more than China and the number of United States children learning piano is only one-sixth of China. The different way of using national resources will have the impact on the growth of the next generation.

This is neither to look down the future of the American people nor to raise the Chinese future position. But remind the leaders of the United States. They should adjust the allocation of their resources in a timely manner.

Spending on military development and ignore the living standard of the people May one day cause the downfall of the United States!

The new elect-president of United States in looking at change of policies should bear in mind to reduce the defense budget. Or else the U.S. children may have to serve coffee for Chinese bosses in 20-30 years time!

16th, December, 2008

美国人要注意

20~30 年后你的孩子将为中国老板端咖啡。

香港《亚洲时报在线》指出美国的国防预算是中国的六倍多，但美国学习钢琴的孩子只有中国的六分之一。资源调配不同将影响下一代的成长。

这不是看低美国人的未来，也不是提高中国人未来的身份，而是提醒美国领导人，应该及时调整资源的分配以免将来变成一个强兵的穷国，把太多钱用在军事上，而忽略了人民的生活质素。

以强调要改变美国而当选的新总统，对美国未来的新国防预算，会不会为了避免二三十年后的美国孩子不必替中国老板端咖啡而有所节制？根据新总统最近的谈话：他决定将把从伊拉克撤退的军队，转移到阿富汗去参战，并声言一定要在阿富汗战胜才收兵。那么新的国防预算，肯定只有增加而没有减少了！

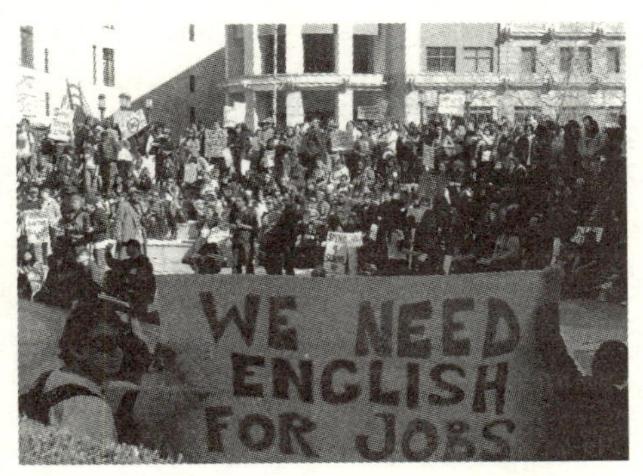

⊙ 美国加州公立学校全州大罢课抗议校方涨学费

写于 2008 年 12 月 16 日

Take and Give!

U.S. treasury international capital flow released the report in September 2008 that China has held United States treasury bonds amounted to 585 billion dollars. It became the United States largest creditor overtaking Japan. . Since the U.S. financial crisis many Chinese has suggested to their government to take this opportunity to bargain with the U.S. for more fairness toward China on the international affairs but Chinese government not only refused to do so. On the contrary, the Chinese government even decided to buy more U.S. bonds in order to raise people confidence on U.S. financial situations and only asked the U.S. government to take good care of China assets security in U.S. Now, the world is watching as how the new U.S. president is going to change his policy toward China. If he is clever enough he should give face to Chinese leaders and stop talking about China human rights record, trade, surplus and military threat etc...All these complaints do not solve the US jobless problems and treasury deficit. In fact, the new President's new policy toward China should consider the followings:

1. Try to make use of China huge treasury reserve and economic development strength to solve its internal financial and economic problems.

2. Make use China good influence and close relationship with most of Asia country to help Americans to be loved instead of hated by people in Asia.

礼尚往来

美国财政部对外公布国际资本流动报告：2008 年 9 月份中国持有美国国债的金额达到 5850 亿美元，超越日本成为美国第一债权人。

自从美国发生金融海啸后，很多中国人主张政府应该利用这个机会和美国讨价还价。在国际事务上，应该获得更合理的待遇。中国政府不但不愿意乘人之危取得利益。相反地，还继续买进大量美国债券，只要求美国要确保中国在美国资产的安全而已。

现在全世界都在关注美国新总统将来如何改变他对中国的政策，如果他够聪明的话，应该考虑到中国领导人的面子问题，不要再对中国的人权记录、贸易出超和军事发展的问题说三道四，有关这方面的指责，对解决美国的失业和赤字难题完全没有帮助。

其实，新的美国总统应该考虑实行下列几个对中国的新政策：

1. 借助中国大量的储备金，以及强大的经济能力缓解其国内的金融和经济难题。

2. 利用中国在亚洲的天时、地利、人和，协助美国减少亚洲人对美国的仇视，以及取得更多亚洲的经济利益。

3. America should not ignore China's need and not to always take without return.

12th, December, 2008

3. 但俗语说"礼尚往来"，美国不要只求单边的利益而忘记对中国的回报。

写于 2008 年 12 月 12 日

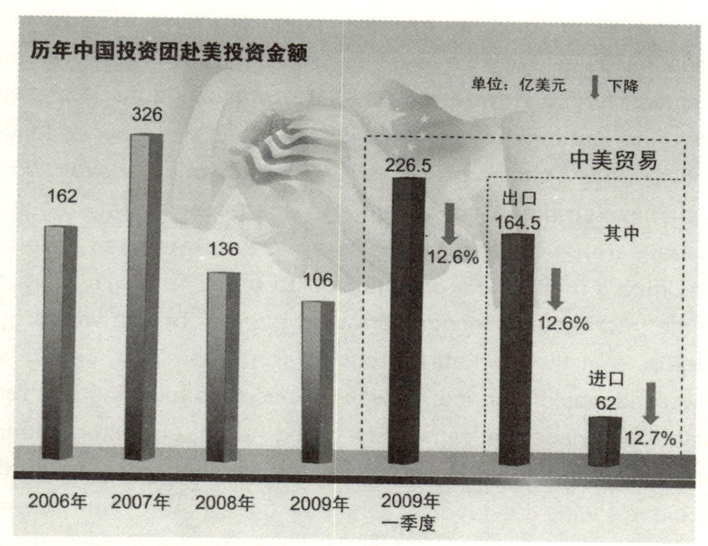

⊙ 历年中国赴美投资金额图表

Taiwan wouldn't progress if independence party is in power!

In power for 8 years, Democratic Progress Party refused to take the ride of China, but advocated “De-China” and independence, so the economic development of Taiwan is swimming against the tide! After assuming office, Ma Ying-jeou administration could not fulfill campaign promises to revive the economy soon, and as a result the polls showed his approval rate has kept falling! However, Ma has never ascribed the economic mess he just took over from DPP to Taiwan pro-independence activists. He promised repeatedly: Taiwan would recover soon. Ma Administration is confident perhaps because they thought if mail, transport and trade links were established, capital of China's mainland were allowed to enter Taiwan's market, some international recognition were gained, Taiwan would get profits from the pockets of tourists from mainland, capital of mainland would rush into Taiwan for business founding and real estate purchase, Taiwan capital could return, and international enterprises would spring up. These expectations may be partly achieved with the favor of Chinese government, but Taiwan independence remains the biggest hurdle for Ma Administration to honor their promises.

According to the polls, more than 20% out of 23 million Taiwan people are pro-independence activists or those who are in favor of them. These 4 million people will lose their reason at anytime to seize on the tragic fate of Chen Shui-bian family and make an issue of it, push Ma administration into unceasing

“台独”不除进步不了！

民进党执政八年，不搭中国顺风车，却要去中独立，使台湾经济逆水行舟！马英九政府上台后，由于没办法兑现竞选诺言，马上把经济搞好，以致民调一路下跌！却不懂得把这个刚接手下来的经济烂摊子归咎于“台独”分子的作乱！只有一再保证：台湾很快便会好起来，马政府的信心来源可能是以为只要搞好三通，开放大陆资金来台投资，争取到一些国际空间，就能够赚到大陆游客的钱，大陆资金也会来台创业买房地产，台资可能回流，国际企业也增加，这些期望，在大陆政府善意协助之下，可能会有些表面化的成果，但“台独”的隐忧，仍是马政府要实现诺言的最大障碍。

根据民调资料，台湾2300万人口中有百分之二十以上是“台独”及亲“台独”分子，这四百多万人，随时会失去理性，将陈水扁家族的悲惨下场借题发挥，给马政府制造没完没了的麻烦，破坏地方的安宁，使旅客裹步，外商不来投资，台商不但不回流，到大陆投资和寻找新商机的人反而会更多，在这种情况下，台湾的经济怎么会好起来呢？

troubles, and undermine local peace, and as a result,less tourists may come to Taiwan,foreign capital would retreat, and Taiwan capital would seek opportunities of investment and doing business in Mainland China rather than return to Taiwan. In this case, how could there be economic prosperity in Taiwan?

Therefore, for the economic boom of Taiwan, a peaceful and stable society is needed. In view of this,the problem of Taiwan independence must be solved in order to build such a social environment. Ma Administration must be in face of the reality, and dare to stress it to 23 million Taiwan people,tell them that the difficulty of Taiwan is caused by minority of people who require Taiwan independence, but if Taiwan people want a better life, higher international status and social security, the idea of Taiwan independence should be eliminated, so as to achieve the reunification with China under favorable preconditions. To be a "China Taiwanese" with high international status, honor, and a promising future, nothing to lose! Moreover, China has declared repeatedly, after the reunification, the assets and fortune of Taiwan remain belonging to Taiwan people, but all the assets of China would be shared with Taiwan people. Taiwan pro-independence activists please don't cling to the daydream which is good to none but worse to yourselves any more!

China's mainland has repeatedly stressed: no matter which party you are from, regardless of what you have said or what you have done, if you as a Taiwan citizen are in favor of "One China", you will be regarded as a family member of China, and you are welcomed to China. This is the toast to those Taiwan pro-independence activists offered by Chinese government. If they are still in illusion, Ma Administration must take some countermeasures, such as:

因此，要搞好台湾的经济，必须先要有一个和平安定的社会环境，而要达到这个目的，就必需先要解决“台独”的问题，马政府应该面对现实，对2300万台湾人民强调：台湾的困境是少数要独立的人所造成的，台湾人要过更好的生活，在国际上有更好的地位和保障，就要排除“台独”的思想，有条件地和大陆统一。做一个有地位、有面子、有前途的“中国台湾人”没有什么不好！何况大陆已一再宣布：统一后台湾的资产和财富不但仍归台湾人所有，大陆的资产和一切所有台湾人都有份，“台独”分子不要死抱着害人害己的梦想了！

大陆再三强调：对台湾人不管他们以前是哪一党哪一派，做什么事说什么话都不会追究，只要他们本着一中的原则，就都是一家人，欢迎他们到大陆看看，这是大陆政府献给广大“台独”份子的“敬酒”，如果“台独”份子仍不清醒，马政府就应该对“台独”份子出台一些“罚酒”的政策，例如：

1. 不同意“一中”的人将不准拥有“中华民国”护照，禁止他们前往大陆，理由是避免他们在大陆做坏事。

2. 所有主张“台独”的人，都必须向政府登记，澄清他们的政治立场。

3. 全台湾所有学校都开始学习简体字和汉语拼音，不及格的学生都不能毕业。

4. 不同意“一中”的电视台、电台和报馆，都不发给营业准证，因为没有国家意识。

5. 国际法理上台湾是中国的领土，宣布不承认是“中国台湾人”的“台独”份子都是非法的台湾居民，如果有人制造纷乱，政府有权把他们赶走。

1. People who don't agree with "One China" will not be allowed to have a ROC passport, and they will not be allowed to go to China's mainland to avoid they would be committing crime there.

2. All those who advocate Taiwan independence have to register their names in the government, to clarify their political stance.

3. In all the schools of Taiwan, simplified Chinese and Chinese pinyin should be included into compulsory lessons, and students who fail in these lessons would not be allowed to graduate.

4. Business license could not be issued to TV stations, broadcast stations and newspapers that are not in favor of "One China", because they don't put the interest of the whole nation to the first place.

5. In international legal principle, Taiwan is the territory of China. Taiwan pro-independence activists, who don't admit that they are "China Taiwanese", are all illegal residents of Taiwan. If they cause any troubles, government can drive them away.

Taiwan is a liberal and democratic "country", but government can legislate to protect the country and the interests of the majority, isolating Taiwan pro-independence activists who do harm to government and people. All the Chinese including overseas Chinese should take on the responsibility to condemn them, because their rebellion makes China's mainland subordinate to western countries and hinder the prosperity of China.

Meanwhile all Chinese people knew that the Taiwan independence movement was encouraged by America indirectly, this wrong policy should stop if American people wish to be loved by the Chinese people.

8th, December, 2008

台湾是自由民主的“国家”，但是政府可以立法保护国家和广大人民的利益，把有害于政府和人民的“台独”份子排除掉。所有中国人包括海外华侨华人都有资格和责任谴责这些“台独”份子，是他们的造反使大陆对西方国家仍要低声下气，阻碍了中国更快步上富强之道。

同时所有中国人都知道台湾的独立运动是受到美国的间接鼓励，美国如果要得到 13 亿中国人的好感，就不应该阻止台湾和中国的统一。

写于 2008 年 12 月 8 日

⊙ 台北大游行民众展示反“独”标语

US Unemployment

The elect President of America has announced that he will create 2.5 million new jobs for the United States in 2 years times. But can he solve the unemployment problems with this effort? The authority concerned should study more carefully the cause of unemployment in order to apply the right medicine.

In 1998 the futurology expert William W Wen indicated in his book (The Future Conquest) that after the year of 2030 the whole world need only 2% the present work force to produce the same amount of production for all people.

If he is correct, the manpower need for the America will be 3% less by every year. His justification is based on the replacement of human power by the advance of science and technology using electronic, computerize automation, robotics etc... Even taxi without driver will be on the road of New York City soon. The increase of US population is also on the high side, due to no birth control and loose immigration policy. In view of this, the followings suggestions should be considered to solve the US jobless problems.

1. Reduce all automated, electronic, computer, robot development and operation

2. shorter working hours and increase people leisure living environment (European countries already have implemented a four-day work week, 8 hours per day system)

3. Control birth rate and immigration

4. Give allowance to Americans to travel abroad or work as

美国失业的原因

美国新总统奥巴马宣布两年内将为美国增加 250 万个新工作机会。此举能够解决美国的失业问题吗？有关当局也许应该关注一些失业的实际因果，才能对症下药！

1998 年未来学专家威廉·W·温辟辛格在他的书《征服未来》中指出："2030 年以后只需要世界现有劳动力的 2% 来进行生产就能满足所有人需要的产品。"

如果他的预计正确，美国每年平均会减少 3% 人力的需要。他的依据可能是基于世界科学技术在不停地进步，部分人力被电子、电脑、自动化、无人化操作和机器人等所代替，纽约州很快就要出现无人驾驶的的士了！更何况还有没有节制的生育和移民使人口增长偏高。

在这种情况之下，奥巴马计划提供的 250 万个新工作机会，恐怕还是很难解决美国的失业问题。

除非美国考虑实行下列几点建议：

1. 停止一切自动化、电子化、电脑化、机器人等的研究和作业。

2. 缩短工作时间，增加人们的休闲生活环境（欧洲有些国家已实行每周工作四天，每天 8 小时的制度）。

3. 有效控制人口增长率和限制移民条例。

4. 津贴美国人出国旅游或当义工（北欧已有国家这样做了）。这种行为不但可以争取世人对美国的好感，也能够让美国人知道世界上还有那么多的穷人需要救济。

volunteers (some countries in Europe have already done so) this will not only gain the appreciation for the Americans from the world. But also to let Americans know that there are still so many poor people in the world need help!

If the unemployment problem cannot be solved, then do not blame that is due to low cost of Chinese imported goods. In fact, the cheap Chinese goods are great help to the lives of Americans especially for poor black in America.

In fact the computer and automation system company are likely to be blame for the cause of high jobless problem that the authority should be concerned of.

25th, November, 2008

如果失业问题解决不了，也不要把原因归咎于便宜的中国进口货。只有便宜的中国进口货，才能减轻美国人的生活负担，尤其是比较贫穷的黑人的生活负担。

其实，电脑公司和生产自动化设备的企业才是造成美国人失业的主要原因之一。因此，要真正解决美国的失业问题就必须认真考虑实行上面的几点建议。

写于 2008 年 11 月 25 日

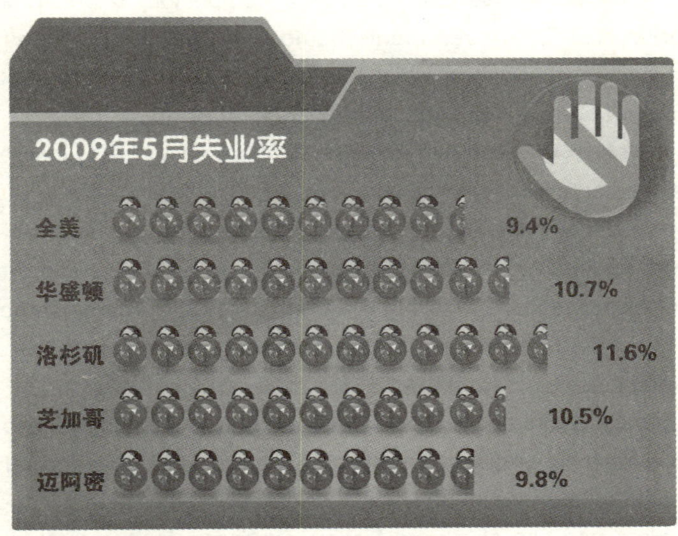

⊙ 美国首都失业率创 25 年来新高

How to save the auto industry?

The three major US auto plants asked the government for $25 billion cash, or else face bankruptcy. The US government is already in trouble because of the financial crisis. Yet another trouble is coming up…, like the Chinese proverb said "under a leaking the rain again!" a multitude of things happen in one roof. How to solve this problem?

The followings suggestions may worth considering:

1. Japan and Germany are strong competitors in the US auto market. The US government should urge the two countries to reduce import of motor vehicles to the US. Since both are the US good alliance nations ought to help each other.

Otherwise US should exercise WTO dumping law to increase the two countries car import duty.

2. Move part of their manufactories plant to developing countries such as China and India etc… in order to reduce the cost of production. This not only enhances the competiveness at home and abroad, it can also preserve the original US car market.

3. Cut production, shorten working hours, give allowances to the remaining workers to work in Chinese car factory, and other emerging countries. In this way, US can solve the unemployment problem and can also earn foreign exchange for the state. It is time for the US to change the reaping without sowing policy.

4. Encourage American to buy only US-made cars, learning

如何救汽车工业

美国三大汽车厂，向政府求救，急需要融资几百亿元，否则将会面临破产。美国政府为了解救金融危机，已经够头痛了，再加上重要的汽车工业也需要救济，有如“屋漏又逢连阴雨”，千头万绪，国会又多了一个难以解决的问题需要讨论——要不要救汽车工厂?！如何解救?！

下列几个解救美国汽车工业的方案，也许值得有关当局考虑：

1. 日本和德国是美国汽车市场最强大的竞争者，美国政府也许可以请求他们站在友好联盟国的立场，自动减少出口到美国的汽车数量，否则将依据世贸倾销法，加重这两个国家的汽车进口税。

2. 一劳永逸，政府协助这些汽车厂把部分设备迁移到中国和印度等发展中国家生产，以便减轻生产成本，不但可以提高竞争能力，也可以保存国内外的原有汽车市场。

3. 减产，缩短工作时间，把剩余技工以津贴方式保送他们到中国等新兴汽车工业国寻找工作机会，不但可以解决失业问题，也可以为国家赚取外汇，改变不劳而获的政策。

4. 鼓励人民尽量购买国产汽车，学习日本人和韩国人

Japanese and Koreans patriotism… do not eat US rice and U.S. beef!

19th, November, 2009

不吃美国米和不吃美国牛肉的爱国精神！

写于2008年11月19日

⊙ 克莱斯勒用汽车拼起“美国国旗”

America should not ignore

Japan rightist people demonstrated in front of the Ministry of Defense to support Air Force General Tamogami who was fired because of his stand that Japan was not the aggressor in World War II!

Many Japanese agreed with him even though China, North and South Korea and other Asian nations still have painful memories of Japan's aggression. These countries have strongly denounced Tamogami's remarks.

10th, November, 2008

美国不可不理

日本右翼人士在国防部外举行集会，声援被开除的田母神俊雄。他是日本空军自卫队总参谋长，坚持日本不是二次大战的侵略者。

很多日本人赞成他的说法，并不顾及中国、朝鲜、韩国、及亚洲另一些国家被日本侵略的痛苦仍记忆犹新的现实，更对强烈否定田母神俊雄的说法。

写于 2009 年 11 月 10 日

⊙ 美国十名老兵参观沈阳二战盟军战俘集中营旧址

Japan Not an Invader in World War II?

It was the chief of the general staff in Japan air force that stressed in his rewarded article.

He put it in his essay "Japan waged the war of aggression against China according to the treaties, and the prosperity and security on the Korean Peninsula were acquired under the colonial rule of Japan." He thought that Japan was involved in the World War II owing to the president of US Roosevelt, who was manipulated by the Communist International at that time. Therefore, Japan was forced to join the war. Besides, he also mentioned that "although so far there are still lots of people holding the view: Japan is 'an invader in big East Asia War', inflicting unbearable suffering on many Asian countries, we must understand one point that many Asian countries view this war in positive way". He pointed out then Japanese governor was even revered by the people from Thailand, Burma, India, Singapore and Indonesia. He alleged that it certainly was a mistaken condemnation to assert Japan was an invader nation.

I made no mistakes to remind the US to be cautious about Japanese thoughts, and please remember the complaints from Japanese: "the participation in World War II was forced by US President Roosevelt?!" It will keep rankling in their mind, so US must look out!

5th November, 2008

日本非二战侵略者?

日本非二战侵略者，这个观点是这位日空军总参谋长，在他得奖的文章中所强调的。

他在文章中写道“日本过去对中国的侵略是按条约行事，而朝鲜半岛在日本的殖民统治下是繁荣和安全的”。他认为日本当年是因美国总统罗斯福才会卷入二战，而罗斯福当时受到了共产国际的操纵，因此，日本参战是迫不得已的。此外，他也提到“至今虽有不少人还是认为：日本是‘大东亚战争的侵略者’，并对亚洲多个国家造成了难以承受的痛苦。但我们必须明白这一点，多个亚洲国家都正面看待这场战争”。他指出，当时的日本统治者甚至还受到泰国、缅甸、印度、新加坡和印度尼西亚等地人民的尊崇。他声称日本是一个侵略者国家肯定是错误的指责。

⊙ 日本侨报社推出第 14 本记录日军侵华罪行的反战图书

我请美国要小心日本人的思想是对的，请记得日本人的抱怨：“日本的参战是被罗斯福总统所迫的！”他们仍在耿耿于怀，因此美国要小心啊！

写于 2008 年 11 月 5 日

Welcome Chinese to the United States!

20-30 years ago, it was difficult for Chinese to go abroad and more difficult if they wish to go to the United States. The reason is that the US government does not want them to work and settle in the US. Now, the US authority should be aware that the Chinese living standard has been greatly improved and more and more Chinese people are getting rich. Therefore there will not be many Chinese people wishing to settle in the US any more. Chinese want to go to US for

1.) Post graduate studies 2.) Tourists 3.) Business

In view of this the US government must start to open door to welcome the Chinese visitors. Thus, US will surely gain enormous benefit from these Chinese visitors. In particular, rich tourists may be the way home in the United States if the United States Government can introduce some new policies (for example to those who have purchase more than 1million US$ and above US properties will be entitled to be resident in the US and so on). Gradually this could be one of unexpected great revenue for the United States to help rescue the financial crisis and ease the glooming property market.

Therefore, Welcome Chinese to the United States should be the priority of United States.

31st, October, 2008

欢迎中国人

20~30 年前，中国人出国难！要到美国更难！现在中国人出国已经很方便了，但美国对中国人入境的大门仍关得很紧，因为担心中国人到美国工作和定居。

美国有关当局应该知道，现在中国人的生活，已经大大改善了，富裕的中国人也已经很多了，要到美国工作和定居的人已经不多了，现在要到美国的中国人应该只有三个大类：1. 到美国留学深造的学生；2. 旅游观光客；3. 寻找投资机会的商人。

因此，一向以国家利益为重的美国政府，应该开始争取中国人到访，对中国人应该大开方便之门，美国肯定将会从大量到访的中国人中获得无穷尽的经济利益，尤其是富有的游客可能会顺便在美国置业。如果美国政府能够出台一些新政策，例如：凡购置产业超过 100 万美元者，将可以获得居留权等。这将会为美国提供一条巨大的财路，对解救美国目前楼市的困境将有意想不到的帮助！

因此，欢迎中国人到美国应该是美国政策应该优先考虑的问题。

⊙ 中国中产阶层已成海外移民主力

写于 2008 年 10 月 31 日

The United States should cut and save!

The United States Congress has passed US $700 billion to rescue the current financial crisis, President Bush has assured the world that the financial crisis will be resolved, But Wall Street continues to decline in the index!

Because the fund can only be stopgap measures to rescue the market, the main problem is with the richest countries in the world has become the world's largest debtor nation, since the country is too expensive!

The following figure is likely to cause the world to have less confidence on the US financial position. According to the national debt clock in New York, October 19, 2008 records, the U.S. debt index is $ 10 trillion. Base on 300 million population of the United States to an average share of each citizen the liability is 34,000 U.S. dollars. (since September 28, 2007 from the daily increase in liabilities was 3.45 billion U.S. dollars.) In principle, the U.S. could be bankrupt at any time, if all the debtors wish to withdraw all their money.

Therefore, in order to win the world's confidence, the US government should seriously consider reducing the budget deficit and national liabilities greatly.... this is the right solution to solve the financial crisis. The United States should make known to the world that they have decided to implement the following policies:

1. No longer spend money on building the military. The existing U.S. military capabilities have been regarded as a world's best. It is already a Superpower. No country in the world will dare

美国应该节流救市

美国应该节流救市！

尽管美国国会已经通过 7000 亿元救市基金，布什总统也不断保证金融危机将会解决，但华尔街的指数仍不停下滑！

因为救市基金只能治标，主要问题出在世界最富有的国家已经变成世界最大的负债国，国家开销太大所致！

下面的数字可能就是造成世人对美国财务情况失去信心的主要原因。根据纽约国家负债指数 2008 年 10 月 19 日的记录，美国负债指数是：$ 10 trillion（已超过 10 万亿美元，非常严重）。

以美国 3 亿人口计算，平均每人要分摊的负债额是 34000 美元，自 2007 年 9 月 28 日起每天增加的负债是 3.45 亿美元。

理论上美国会随时破产，如果所有债主要取回存款的话。

因此，为争取世人的信心，美国应该认真地考虑设法大量减少预算赤字和国家负债，这才是正确解决财务危机的办法，因此美国应该向世界宣布决定实行下列政策：

1. 不再花钱发展军事设备，以美国现有的军事能力已经算是世界超强国了，安全已经有保证，世界任何一个国家不会也不想攻击美国。

2. 不要用武力强迫他国改变立场，例如伊拉克战争，

to attack the United States.

2. Do not use force to change other countries position, such as the war in Iraq. The United States is spending hundreds of billions of money at the expense of the lives of so many people, but ending with no results ...Iraq's people want the US to withdraw its troops from Iraq as early as possible!

3. Do not spend money to protect the security of other countries and to withdraw of all military bases in the world, it will not only reduce the large number of military spending, but could also win the goodwill of the people of the world.

4. Do not rely on foreign imports oil. It will save large sums of money and can also avoid the conflict with unfriendly oil-producing countries; to implement the oil self-sufficiency policy is a positive direction.

US should implement the above mentioned policy in order to solve the financial crisis effectively.

27th, October, 2008

美国花了几千亿的钱，牺牲了那么多人的生命，结果不但得不到伊拉克的友谊，他们的人民已开始要美国撤军了！

3. 不要再花钱保护别国的安全，撤回分布在全世界的军事基地，不但可以减轻大量军事开销，也可以赢得世人的好感。

4. 不要再依靠进口外国石油，不但可以节省巨额金钱，也可以减少和不友好的产油国发生摩擦。实行国内用油自给自足的政策。

上面是美国应该实行的重要节流政策，以便达到救市的目的。

写于 2008 年 10 月 27 日

⊙ 美将拿 1000 亿资金吸收金融机构“有毒”资产

About US-India nuclear deal

Report from Washington: In a high-profile ceremony United State President George W Bush signed a land mark US-India nuclear agreement at the White House. Mr. Bush and Indian Prime Minister first agreed to it in July 2005. But earlier on ran into objections from critics who were worried about the spread of nuclear know -how.

The agreement lifted a ban on civilian nuclear trade imposed after India first conducted a nuclear test. Explode in 1974. It also offers India access to sophisticated US technology and cheap atomic energy, in return for New Delhi allowing U.N. inspection of some of its civilian nuclear facilities.

US have won the approval for the deal from the international Atomic Energy Agency the United Nations Nuclear watchdog, and the Nuclear Suppliers Group which controls global atomic trade. The reasons for the US to convince the United Nations Nuclear authorities to approve the India deal are: "This Legislation will strengthen our global nuclear nonproliferation efforts, protect the environment, create jobs and assist India in meeting its growing energy needs in a responsible manner."

But from the high profile ceremony presented by President Bush, one can see obviously that the reasons behind. The US wanted to please India..., to do India a favor in order to win India to stand closer to the US on the international affairs.

However, since the US and India nuclear agreement deal is not concerned about the spread of nuclear know –how...Then

关于美印核合作协议

来自华盛顿的报告：美国总统布什以一种高姿态在白宫签署了一项特殊的美印核合作协议。布什总统和印度总理早在 2005 年 7 月就已经同意了这个协议，但是因为被反对者批评，担心将造成核武器扩散而搁置。

这次美印核合作协议，取消了印度民间不可进行核能源贸易的禁令（这条禁令是针对 1974 年印度首次进行核试爆后实施的），协议也允许让印度获得美国的先进技术和廉价的原子能，换取新德里允许联合国检查他的一些民用核设施。

美国已经从国际原子能机构获得包括联合国核监督和全球核供应原子贸易，控制集团等有关方面的同意。美国用以说服联合国当局批准美印核能协议的理由是："这项协议将加强全球防核扩散的努力、保护环境、创造就业机会，并协助印度满足其日益增长的能源需求，以负责任的态度发展。"

但是从美国总统布什高姿态出席这次核协议的仪式，人们可以看到很明显的原因是美国想讨好印度，让印度在核协议事件得到所需，以便赢得印度在国际事务上更接近美国。

既然美国和印度所签的核能协议可以不担心有核武器扩散的可能性，美国应该考虑提供同样的条件，供应其他有同样需求的国家，这是一个顺理成章的机会，不但可以

US should consider to offer the same deal to other countries who need it and this is a good chance for US to make good money and win good relationships. It is a very feasible policy that US leaders should consider.

For example, Iran and US are in big argument on nuclear testing. Iran insisted that they just wanted to produce nuclear energy only. In view of this US should try to offer Iran the same terms and conditions that offer to India, in order to resolve the hostility between two countries peacefully. Save the world from another tragedy fighting!

26th, October, 2008

为美国赚取金钱，还可以赢得良好的国际关系。这是一个非常可行的政策，很值得美国领导人来考虑。

例如：伊朗和美国在核试验问题上的争论，伊朗坚持他们搞核试，只是想生产核能源而已。因此美国应该尝试和伊朗谈判，以同样的条件和伊朗签订协议，以解决两国之间的敌意，避免另一场影响国际和平的悲惨战斗！

写于 2008 年 10 月 26 日

⊙ **共同关注**

Be Careful of the Japanese Thinking!

America atomic bomb exploded at Hiroshima and Nagasaki on August 6, 1945 has stop the world war II and a few hundred thousand of Japanese died in this tragedy!

However, kind America is helping Japan to be one of the world's stronger economic and military powers. By right, the Japanese should be very happy with their present position. Japanese should bear in mind that without America tolerant policy they will not be able to recover so fast from the war as a defeated country. The Japanese should also remember how many Pacific Regional people have been killed in the war created by them. But the Japanese cannot forget the American bombs on Hiroshima and Nagasaki and are not grateful to the good help of America.

One can see very often that is demonstration against America military base in Japan and evidence proved that the Cabinet of Japanese government is in favor of worshiping at the Yasukuni Shrina longer than those do not.

From these events, one can see the majority of Japanese are still very much in favor admiring their war hero. Therefore, they don't want American military base in Japan to keep an eye on them. And they are eager to build up their military power quietly. America should be careful of the Japanese thinking.

In view of this American leaders should be clever enough, not to help Japan to build up their military power any more. Otherwise, another attack like Pearl Harbor may happen one day who know?

要小心日本人的思想

美国原子弹于1945年8月6日在广岛和长崎爆炸，加速了第二次世界大战的结束，却使几十万日本人死于这场悲剧！

然而，美国却帮助日本成为世界经济和军事强国，有得有失。日本也许应该很满意他们目前的现状，并且应该牢记，没有美国宽容的政策，他们将不能够这么快从一个战败国成为一个强国。日本人也应该要记得很多太平洋区域人民在战争中被他们杀害。但是，日本似乎不能忘记美国原子弹在广岛和长崎的爆炸，对美国的协助好像不太领情?

我们可以经常看到很多日本人抗议和示威，反对政府让美国在日本建立军事基地。日本内阁领袖如果主张崇拜靖国神社者，就可获得人民的支持，执政时间就会更长。

从这些事件中，人们可以看到，绝大多数日本人仍然非常怀念和崇拜他们的战争英雄。因此，他们不希望美军基地在日本看住他们。他们渴望悄悄地建立自己的军事实力，美国应该小心日本人的想法。

因此美国领导人应该聪明些，不可以再帮助日本增加他们的军事实力了。否则，再次遭遇到袭击珍珠港一样的事件的可能性还是有的，谁知道呢?！

The Pacific regional people especially those have been living under the Japan occupation would be very happy if America can convince Japan not to create any more war in this region and advise them there are many Pacific regional countries people who are still very worried of the Japanese's bellicose manner.

25th, October, 2008

太平洋区域的人，尤其是那些一直生活在日本占领区的人将会非常高兴，如果美国能够说服日本不要在这里制造任何更多的战争，并提醒他们，有很多亚太地区国家的人还非常担心日本的好战主义。

写于 2008 年 10 月 25 日

⊙ 日本部分地方议员参拜靖国神社

Forget and Forgive

Since New York World Trade Twin Towers was destroyed by terrorist on September 11, 2001. America has exerted extra ordinary efforts to capture the terrorist leaders. But after seven years of worldwide tracking, they could not find "Osama Bin Laden",but caused so much inconvenience to the worldwide travelers with their tight security check on air, sea and land travel. This has made so many American and European airline travel agents lose money. Some had gone bankrupt!

Most of the nine hundred million Muslims in the world are unhappy with America.... because America always keeps a suspicious eye on them to see if they are terrorists.

Therefore it's the wrong way to find terrorist, to fight terrorist, and to solve the terrorist problems. I think America should consider to let gone by gone, try to forget 9.11 tragedy and forgive those criminals, in order to win back the hearts of nine hundred million Muslims ... let them alone. Don't try to sell freedom, democracy and human rights to them... if they don't want to buy.

In Chinese, it has been said "Good man scare to fight with bad man. Bad man is scare to fight with the man who does not scare of die." It's not worth for the super power countries to fight with those dare to die man. Otherwise, there will be more and more Muslim become dares to die man! And the suicide booming or "hit and run" games will be without end.

忘记和原谅

自纽约世贸双塔被“恐怖主义”摧毁于2001年9月11日之后，美国付出了巨大的财力，追捕恐怖头目本·拉登，但经过七年的全球搜索，仍没办法捉到，却给世界旅客造成了很多不方便。更甚者，由于在世界各地对旅客进行严密的保安检查，旅客为避免麻烦而减少旅行，结果使许多美国和欧洲的航空公司和旅行社赔钱，有些公司已经宣告破产。

世界9亿穆斯林人，大多数在各地旅行都有过不愉快的感受，因为美国始终保持一种可疑的眼光盯着他们，看看他们是否是恐怖分子。这是寻找恐怖分子及消灭恐怖分子的政策。

我认为，要解决恐怖分子问题，美国应该考虑让过去成为过去，试图忘记911的悲剧和原谅那些罪犯，为了减少穆斯林人的仇恨，最好让他们保持现状。不要试图出售自由、民主和人权给他们，如果他们不想买的话。

中国有句话说：“软的怕硬的，硬的怕横的，横的怕愣的，愣的怕不要命的。”所以美国不应该与不要命的人斗争，否则，将会有越来越多的穆斯林人成为不怕死的人！制造更多自杀式或“打了就跑”的惨剧。

The Chinese proverb said “Better to dissolve the hatred rather than deepen it!” The America and western countries leaders should learn this proverb and review the fighting terrorist policy.

25th, October, 2008

中国的谚语说:"冤家宜解不宜结!"美国和西方国家领导人应该领悟这个谚语的意思，改变打击恐怖主义的政策。

写于 2008 年 10 月 25 日

⊙ 美国世贸中心被两架飞机撞击后发生强烈爆炸

Learn from Tony Blair

The former prime minster of Great Britain Mr. Tony Blair said "we can help China embrace the future" in his article published in the Wall Street Journal on August 26, 2008.

Mr. Tony Blair's appraisal of China nobody can stop the sifting of tremendous development and power to Asia. I would like to quote part of his article for Americans friends to read and learn as how a top western politician sees a new China.

He said "The Beijing Olympic Games were a powerful spectacle, stunning in sight and sound ...... an open up of China that can never be reserved, it also means that ignorance and fear of China will steadily decline as the reality of modern China becomes more apparent power and influence is shifting to the east......

During my 10 years as British leader, I could see the accelerating pace of China's continued emergence as a major power...... Since leaving office I have visited four times and will shortly return again...... The whole feel of the city was a world away from the China. I remember on my first visit 20 years ago and the people are proud, really and honestly proud of their country and its progress......

China is now a major global player, so whether the issue is climate change ......we need China to be constructive; we need it to be using its power in partnership with us. None of this means we shouldn't continue to raise the issues of human rights, religious freedoms and democratic reforms as European and

学习英国首相布莱尔

前任英国首相托尼·布莱尔先生说:“我们可以帮助中国拥抱未来。”他的文章刊登在2008年8月26日的华尔街日报上。

托尼·布莱尔先生指出，没有任何力量能够阻挡中国成为亚洲的强大国家。我想引用一部分他的文章，请美国朋友阅读和了解一个西方的政治家如何看待一个新中国的崛起。

他说:“北京奥运会的场面非常宏大，有着惊人的视觉效果和声音效果。一个开放的中国永远不会停止发展，这也意味着无知和恐惧中国的人要逐渐面对现实，一个现代化的中国已经扎根东方!

我当英国领导人10年以来，看到了中国逐渐发展成为一个强大的国家，自从上任后，我本人先后访问了中国4次，不久将会再次访问，现在看中国整个感觉好像是另一个世界。我记得我20年前第一次访问中国时，其人民都为自己国家的进步而感到非常自豪和骄傲。

中国现在是一个重要的全球性的成员，所以不管气候如何变化，我们需要一个建设性的中国，我们需要她利用其权利与我们合作。因此，这意味着我们不应该继续提起人权的问题及宗教信仰自由化民主的改革政策。

American leaders have done in recent weeks......

Personally, I think it will be incredibly enriching. New experiences; new ways of thinking liberate creative energy...... For the next U.S. president; this will be or should be at the very top of the agenda......

And we should learn from and respect each other. That is the way of the 21st century."

In this regard, the Americans press should take the initiative steps to make the American politics leaders learn from Mr. Tony Blair to see the facts and true of China situation correctly. For the benefit of their nation and building good relationship for Sino- US if the America really wanted to be loved by the Chinese people.

24th, October, 2008

就个人而言，我认为这将是难以置信的进步，从新的经验、新的思维方式中解放出来的创造力，对于下一任美国总统，这将是或应该是最优先的议程。

我们应该学习如何相互尊重，这就是21世纪。"

关于这方面，美国媒体应采取主动步骤，促进美国政治领袖学习托尼·布莱尔先生看到的事实，以便有利于和中国建立起良好的关系，如果美国真的想得到中国人的喜欢的话。

写于2008年10月24日

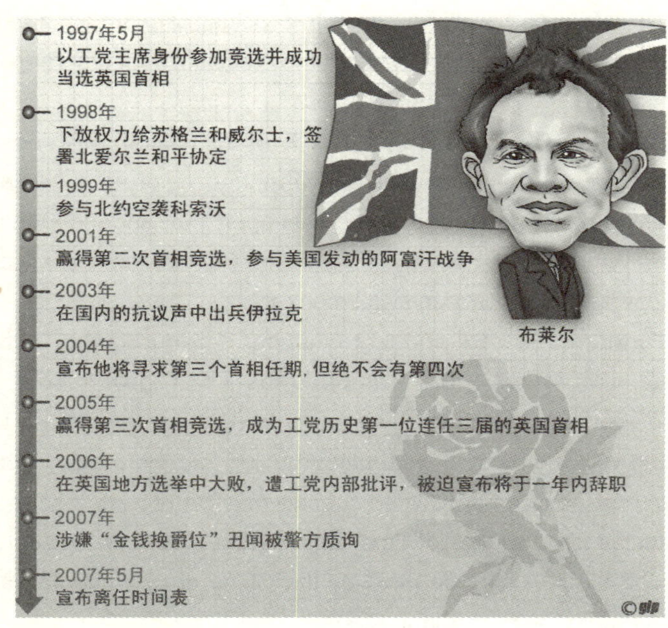

1997年5月
以工党主席身份参加竞选并成功当选英国首相
1998年
下放权力给苏格兰和威尔士，签署北爱尔兰和平协定
1999年
参与北约空袭科索沃
2001年
赢得第二次首相竞选，参与美国发动的阿富汗战争
2003年
在国内的抗议声中出兵伊拉克
2004年
宣布他将寻求第三个首相任期，但绝不会有第四次
2005年
赢得第三次首相竞选，成为工党历史第一位连任三届的英国首相
2006年
在英国地方选举中大败，遭工党内部批评，被迫宣布将于一年内辞职
2007年
涉嫌"金钱换爵位"丑闻被警方质询
2007年5月
宣布离任时间表
布莱尔
©gip

⊙ 布莱尔执政十年大事记

Protect Taiwan: Lose more and gain less

The whole world knew that Taiwan belongs to China. But USA has passed a law to protect Taiwan for the interest of the nation in order to sale weapons to Taiwan to prevent communism from spreading over to the whole pacific region from China.

But time has changed since the Deng Xiaoping decided to open China door to the world up to nowadays. We can see very clearly that China is no longer a closed state.

Therefore it's time for America to consider carrying out a new policy toward China otherwise USA may result in a lost more gain less situation.

Because there are only 10-20% of 23 million Taiwanese people may be happy with USA continued to protect Taiwan and sell arms to Taiwan in order to support their independence dream. Whereas the majority of 1.3 billion Chinese people will be unhappy with America's unlawful manner.

Furthermore, USA should remember that during the China internal war, America fully supported the K.M.T. government. It was given large number of weapons to fight communist party. But end with the most of weapons dropping into the hands of the communist government. This situation may be repeated sooner or later as it's a matter of time only. All the high-tech weapons provided by USA may be used by the China army when Taiwan has its reunion with mainland China.

保护台湾，失多于得！

整个世界都知道，台湾是属于中国的。但是，美国却通过了一项法律，以保护台湾为自己国家牟利，并出售武器给台湾，以防止共产主义从中国扩散到整个亚太地区。

但势易时移，自从邓小平决定打开中国大门向世界开放市场至今，我们已经可以很清楚地看到，中国已不再是一个落后封闭的国家。

因此，美国应重新考虑实行对台湾的新政策，否则美国可能将在中国失去更多的收益。

目前 2300 万台湾人民中，只有 10%~20% 的人可能会很乐意见到美国继续保护台湾，向台湾出售武器，以支持其独立的梦想。但将有 13 亿中国人民对美国保护台湾的政策非常不满。

美国也许应该记得，在中国的内部战争，美国是全力支持国民党政府的。给国民党政府提供大量的武器打击共产党，但结果却有大部分武器落入共产党政府手里。这种情况可能会重复，只是时间问题，当两岸统一时，美国所提供给台湾所有的高科技武器可能会落入中国军队手中。

The American leaders should think carefully and cleverly what is lost and what is gain for continuing to protect Taiwan and sell weapons to Taiwan.

23rd, October, 2008

美国领导人应该认真想一想，如果继续保护台湾，向台湾出售武器，将会是失多于得。

写于 2008 年 10 月 23 日

⊙ 台北举行反军购要和平集会

FOR SALE ONLY

The United States planed to put up missiles defense battery for its allies countries in Europe, Asia and Australia. Obviously the American intention is to prevent the long range missile attack from Russian and China. Both countries warned that such action will escalate military built-up and create tension.

The United States should concentrate on building its missile defense battery within its own border and not spend money and effort to help other countries in return to get nothing but complain from people of the countries.

I am sure if American can prove that the missile defense battery is effective enough to defend and protect their country eventually there will be a lot country willing buy and pay for it.

As such the US government should keep the missile defense battery system “FOR SALE ONLY”. In this way it could earn the respect of other countries and also make some money. It is a one stone two bird policy worthwhile for the US authority to consider.

21st, October, 2008

只供出售

美国计划提供导弹防御系统给欧洲、亚洲和澳大利亚的盟国。显然，美国的意图是为了防止远程导弹的攻击，俄罗斯和中国两个国家都警告这种行动将使军事竞争升级和制造紧张局势。

美国应专注将其导弹防御系统建造在其自己的国土上，而不是花钱和精力去帮助其他国家，因为得到的只不过是其他国家人民的抱怨。

⊙ 美国国家导弹防御系统将正式启用

我相信，如果美国能证明导弹防御系统是有效的，有足够的防御能力和确保自己国家的安全，最终将会有很多国家愿意出钱向美国购买。

因此，美国政府应该坚持他的导弹防御系统"只供出售"，这样不但可以赢得其他国家的尊重，也能够赚得一些金钱，是一个一石二鸟的政策，很值得美国当局考虑。

写于 2008 年 10 月 21 日

Action to make the world joyful

Rice production could not catch up with the increase of world population. One solution is reducing consumption of rice. One country that is doing this is China. According the USA agriculture department China has reduced rice consumption by 3.9%. As such some countries where rice is the main staple food benefited from China's less consumption of rice policy. This could be one of the reasons why China could be love by people more than America.

The price of oil has jumped five times since 2002....and among the reasons are the American war in Iraq and the troublesome relations of Iran. In this circumstances America could follow the China rice-consumption policy and reduce oil use by 5% (America use about 50% of the oil production in the world). I believe strongly that oil price would surely drop back to reasonable levels. If the america 240 million car owners can make this bit of sacrifice many would benefit and life could be easier. And surely this is a good way to make Americans love by the world.

20th, October, 2008

使世界欢乐的行动！

稻米生产不能赶上世界人口的增加，一种解决办法就是鼓励人民尽量减少吃白米饭，中国就是这样做的国家。根据美国农业部的资料，中国已经减少了 3.9% 的大米消费，这样的做法，使一些主食是大米的国家受益于中国的低消费大米政策。这可能就是中国人比美国人更受世人欢迎的主要原因之一。

2002 年以来，石油价格已经上涨了 5 倍，其原因之一就是美国在伊拉克的战争和与伊朗的紧张关系。在这种情况下，美国可以按照中国减少稻米消费的政策，主动减少使用石油 5%（美国使用 50% 左右的世界石油）。我强烈认为，石油价格肯定会回落到合理的水平上。如果美国两亿四千万汽车的车主能够做出有利于世界人民的行动，肯定能够和中国人一样受到更多人的欢迎。

写于 2008 年 10 月 20 日

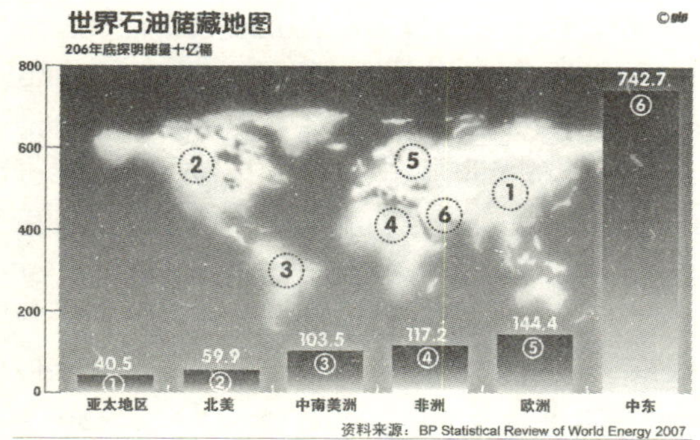

⊙ 世界石油储藏地图

Don't protest anymore!

China has protested against the sale of US arms to Taiwan for 30 years. Nevertheless, the United States continued to sell weapons to Taiwan with a total amount of more than 30 billion U.S. dollars!

Recently, the U.S. government is preparing to approve the sale of a new batch of weapons to Taiwan amidst an improved cross-strait relationship with China. In this period of warmer friendship and cooperation between Sino-US, the United States persistence on selling arms to Taiwan is unconceivable and "If this can be tolerated, what is not!"

As a result, many Chinese scholars had suggested that the authority concerns should take retaliatory measures toward the U.S. for selling arms to Taiwan. The measures should include selling arms to potential US rival and unfriendly forces.

I think China should "retreat in order to advance!" Protesting against US bring little results, on contrary, China should embraces the United States to sell large amount of weapon to Taiwan. Remember, these weapons will sooner or later falls in the hand of the Chinese. Just like the China civil war, the American, through the nationalist government has given a large number of weapons to the Chinese communist's party. This lesson should never be forgotten and the American should be looking out for themselves!

There is a Chinese saying, "To get rid of the bell, one should tackle the bell handle". China should protests against Taiwan; a

不要再抗议了！

中国对美国售卖军备给台湾的事已经抗议了30年，但30年以来，美国仍不断卖武器给台湾，总共超过300亿美元！

据报道，最近美国政府可能又要再批准售卖一批新的武器给台湾了！正当台海两岸关系大为缓和，中美大谈友好合作之际，美国仍坚持要继续卖军备给台湾，真是：是可忍，孰不可忍！

一些中国学者，建议官方对美国售台武器的立场，采取报复措施，包括向美国潜在对手出售武器等。

我认为中国也许应该以退为进，不要再对美国提出没有效果的抗议了！相反地，应该表示欢迎美国继续卖大量武器给台湾，但提醒美国这些武器迟早都将变为中国所有。正如国共内战时美国通过国民党政府输送了大量武器给中共的例子一样。美国不要忘记这个教训，应该好自为之。

解铃还需系铃人！中国要抗议的对象应该是自家人的台湾，严厉警告台湾执政当局，如果继续向美国购买武器，就说明台湾没有诚意以和平理念解决两岸问题，台湾既然有大量财力购买武器，中国就不必对台湾提供优惠贸易政

stern warning should be given to Taiwan authority. Taiwan must prove that they are sincere in resolving the cross-strait issues peacefully and stop buying weapons from the US. Since Taiwan has abundant resources to purchase these weapons, China will not have to offer concessions on Taiwan trade policy. The future of Taiwan will depend on the present course taken by its people.

If the U.S. government has to sell weapons to Taiwan to satisfy the US arms manufacturers, the target customers should be China. President Barack Obama must be smart enough to explore this potential money making trade.

To reduce the U.S. fiscal deficit, to improve Sino-U.S. trade imbalance, the U.S. should open the sale of high-tech and military equipment to china. By far, this is the best policy the U.S. government should implement.

19th, January, 2009

策。台湾人民未来的生活困境将是咎由自取。

若美国政府决定再售卖武器给台湾是为了要满足武器制造商的要求，那中国才是美国军备的超级大顾客。聪明的美国总统奥巴马什么时候才要打开这条巨大的财路呢?

要减少美国大量的财政赤字，要改善中美不平衡的贸易。美国应该开放售卖高科技和军事设备给中国，这才是美国应实行的上策。

写于 2010 年 1 月 19 日

⊙ 美军 F-117 隐形战斗机

Don't force North Korea!

"Don't force the dog to jump the wall"! this is the translation from a Chinese proverb which means to avoid a bite by the dog.

Recently, North Korea conducted nuclear test and made the world worried. America urged the U. N. to impose serious sanction against North Korea. Leaders of United States also warned that, if the security of the U.S. and its Asia allies are threatened or attacked by the North Korea. United States pledges to respond quickly to protect South Korea and Japan.

However, the clever American leaders may have to change and implement new policy toward North Korea, since economic sanction and military threats do not stop North Korea having their nuclear weapons. Don't force North Korea! Instead the United States leaders should consider the following new policy to solve the conflict with North Korea nuclear test issue.

1. To renounce that United States will not prevent North Korea from nuclear test anymore and whether the Korean Peninsula should be a nuclear-free zone or not to let the countries within the area make their own decision.Hence,South Korea may use the kindness and wealth power to persuade North Korea not to fight with South Korea, China may use their influence to urged North Korea to do the right thing in harmony with world.

2. The United States not only have thousands of nuclear bombs also but have a system to block the attack of nuclear bomb. Therefore even if North Korea got their nuclear bomb it may not be able to attack the United States. Only if America is not

不要把人逼急了!

中国俗话说:“不要把人逼急了!”以免被狠狠反击!

朝鲜最近不断进行核试,使美国极度不安,除了要求联合国对朝鲜实行更严厉制裁之外,国家领导人都纷纷警告朝鲜,如果美国和亚洲盟国的安全受到威胁或遭到袭击,美国将会迅速还击,履行保护韩国、日本的诺言。

聪明的美国领导人,对付朝鲜的政策也许要有所改变了,经济制裁和武力威胁,既然改变不了朝鲜要拥有核弹的决心,最好不要再把朝鲜逼急了!下列一些新政策也许值得美国领导人加以考虑实行:

1. 声明放弃阻止朝鲜进行核试,朝鲜半岛要不要成为无核区,请该地区各国自行处理之,韩国可以以亲情和利诱劝说南北双方不要互相残杀,中国可以晓以大义劝朝鲜与世界和谐相处。

2. 美国不但拥有几千枚核弹,并且已有阻挡核弹袭击的设备,朝鲜就算拥有了核弹,也不一定有能力可以发射到美国。只要不怕朝鲜拥有核弹,就可以消除朝鲜要以核弹威胁美国,以达到和美国讨价还价的目的。

afraid of North Korea's possession of nuclear bombs, then North Korea will have less bargaining power with America.

3. To withdraw all U.S. troops stationed in South Korea to make North Korea no excuse to make incidents and South Korea should share their economic wealth with North Korea in order to make one Korea possible...After their unity the United States will able to lest worried of North Korea nuclear threat.

16th, June, 2009

3. 撤走美国驻韩国军队，使朝鲜没有借口可以制造事件，劝韩国把经济成就与朝鲜分享，就容易达到统一的目的，统一之后美国就可以解除朝鲜核弹之忧。

写于 2009 年 6 月 16 日

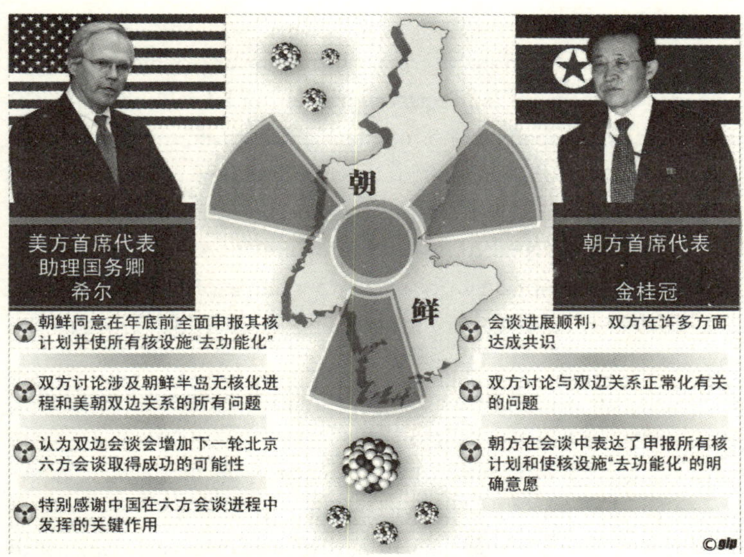

朝
鲜
美方首席代表
助理国务卿
希尔
朝方首席代表
金桂冠
朝鲜同意在年底前全面申报其核计划并使所有核设施“去功能化”
双方讨论涉及朝鲜半岛无核化进程和美朝双边关系的所有问题
认为双边会谈会增加下一轮北京六方会谈取得成功的可能性
特别感谢中国在六方会谈进程中发挥的关键作用
会谈进展顺利，双方在许多方面达成共识
双方讨论与双边关系正常化有关的问题
朝方在会谈中表达了申报所有核计划和使核设施“去功能化”的明确意愿
©gip

⊙ 朝鲜同意解决核计划与核设施“去功能化”问题

Sale of Aircraft Carrier to China

According to the U.S. Navy Times website on January 4, 2008, there are many members of Congress who feel that the U.S. aircraft carrier current force structure is the product of the cold war, not suitable for the new international situation. 11 aircraft carriers are obviously too many! The USA may need only 7 aircraft carriers.

This figure is more than the total number owned by other nations. The cost for an aircraft carrier is from 4 to 10 billion USD and the cost to operate and maintain a heavy aircraft carrier fleet is about 1.5billion per year. If a wise decision could be made by the Congress to reduce the fleet of aircraft carriers from 11 to 7 and the remaining of 4 carriers offer to sell to China, the government will not only get an extra income of billions of dollar but could also save a lot of military spending. There are also the following benefits:

1. There is no permanent enemy in the world! The United States has established diplomatic relation with China 30 years ago. So far it has proven to turn hostility into friendship. When China is in need of their own aircraft carrier the United States should take the initiative step to offer to China to buy over these 4 carriers. If the terms and conditions are reasonable, China may be pleased to accept the offer with much goodwill in return.

2. Let China own USA made aircraft carriers. The U.S. may have less worry that China has some unknown and better aircraft carrier from somewhere else. Through this friendly deal, China

多余航母卖给中国

据美国海军时报网站2008年1月4日援引来自国会的文件称：有很多国会议员认为美国目前的航母部队结构是冷战的产物，不适合新的国际形势，11艘航母显然太多了……这个数字比目前其他国家拥有的航母数量的总和还多，美国或许只需要7艘航母。

美国每艘航母的造价由几十亿美元到100亿美元以上，重型航母编队1年的运行、维护费用为15亿美元，明智的国会如果决定将其拥有的航母队减为7艘，而将剩余的4艘售卖给中国，不但将有几百亿美元的额外收入、减少大量的军事开支，还有下列几点好处：

1. 世界上没有永久的敌国，中美建交迄今30年，已证明可以化敌为友，而当中国正需要建造自己航母的时候，主动协助中国拥有寻求中的航母，肯定会得到中国相当友好的回报。

2. 让中国拥有性能一清二楚的航母，不但不必担心中国可能拥有比自己性能更好的航母，也可以通过友好合作，分担美国单独维护世界和平的任务。

may be able to safe guard the world with United States and save costs for America doing it alone.

3. To delay China's pace of self-made aircraft carrier development and to avoid the China- made aircraft carrier selling to other countries.

4. If the two super power countries in the world can have friendly cooperation in the military field instead of being confrontational, America will be able to save a lot of money from military spending. It's very good for U.S. government and the people.

The general public may think this suggestion is a kind of joke. However it is worthwhile for the new President to take this into consideration as he wants to change US policy.

7th, January, 2009

3. 可以延缓中国自造航母的发展速度，避免中国太快把性能好、造价便宜的航母卖给其他国家，打破美国航母的独大局面。

4. 两个大国如果在军事上能够友好合作，不搞对抗，共同维护世界和平，减少美国的军事开销，对美国政府和人民都有好处。

这个主张一般人可能认为是在开玩笑。但很值得要改变美国政策的新总统加以考虑的。

写于 2009 年 1 月 7 日

⊙ 美国航母“尼米兹”号战斗群抵港短暂停留

The Promotion of Human Rights Policy

The U.S. Congress and Senate House of Representative voted a resolution in majority to call on China to stop repression in Tibet. Meanwhile the White House State Council also expressed concern over human rights question in Tibet. These issues caused aroused strong protests from Beijing. Tibet is an inalienable part of China and US should stay completely out of China's internal affairs. The United States should respect the Chinese people in safeguarding the position of national sovereignty and territorial integrity.

Obviously, this is the worthless policy for United States to interfere with other country internal affairs. Any country regardless of status will not accept any interference by outsiders. President Obama keeps saying that he will change the wrong policies of the United States but take no heed to this. He not only failed to persuade Congress to cease this wrong conduct but even emphasize that this is one of the most important foreign policy of the United States. It is regrettable.... The United States will therefore suffer more resentment of foreigners.

In early years when China was initially governed by the Communist party, the United States wanted to use the Dalai Lama to cause trouble to China and the Dalai Lama also hoped that through the help of the United States may able to return to Tibet one day both sides make used each other is beyond reproach. But the situation changed fast than the people can foresee China after 30 years of economic reforms and became

推广人权的政策

美国国会众议院以绝大多数通过决议案："呼吁中国停止在西藏进行镇压行动。"白宫和国务院也对西藏的人权问题表示关注，引起北京的强烈抗议，并指出："西藏是中国领土不可分割的一部分，西藏事务完全是中国内政，美国应该尊重中国人民维护国家主权和领土完整的立场。"

美国奥巴马总统的回应是："推广人权是美国外交政策中至关重要的一环，希望中国政府和达赖喇嘛展开谈判。"

很明显地这是美国干涉他国内政的下策，任何一个国家不管人权事况如何，都不会接受外国的干涉政策。奥巴马总统口口声声主张要改变美国的错误政策，但对这个公开侵犯他国的立场，不但没有劝国会停止进行，还强调这是美国最重要的外交政策之一环！非常令人遗憾！美国将会因此而树立更多不友好的国家，以及遭受到更多外国人的反感。

昔年，中共执政初期，美国想利用达赖喇嘛给共产主义的中国制造麻烦，达赖喇嘛也希望通过美国的帮助，有朝一日能重新回到西藏，双方互相利用无可厚非。但形势比人强，中国经济改革开放之后，30 年以来国家经济的发展突飞猛进，中美的关系已经发展到互相依靠的地步，达赖喇嘛对美国已经没有利用的价值了，美国为什么还要睁着眼睛说瞎话！把中国要管理好西藏治安的措施，说成是对西藏人民的镇压。无视西藏的进步和开放，是美国最大

one of the economic super power in the world. The Sino-US relations had developed to the stage to rely on each other made the Dalai Lama have no more value to the United States and why should the America still said "Blind word" with opening eye? Blames the security measures in Tibet by China are the suppression on Tibetans ignore the progress and development of Tibet this is a big mistake of United States. The U.S. congress accusing China deliberately and adopted a resolution is aimed to forcing China to give Dalia Lama a way out, but Dalai Lama then open his big mouth to ask China for a pure high degree of autonomy for Tibetans including Qinghai, Gansu, Sichuan, Yunnan Tibetans living in these city his demands are too much unrealistic. In fact, America should advise him to take whatever he can.

The smart American politicians, can always investigate the world human rights situation for each country, but there is no need to use unfriendly words and deeds and legislative to interference other country internal affairs, this is absolutely the wrong approach. Should the United States intended to promote human rights to the world then must first set a good example by their own human rights situation to achieve zero disadvantage, then use the good example with friendly attitude to invite other countries to learn from the United States, this is the correct policy to promote human rights.

23rd, March, 2009

的错误。国会故意通过指责中国的决议，可能是要迫中共给达赖喇嘛一条生路？但达赖喇嘛却借势向中共开大口，要一个纯西藏人的高度大自治区，包括青海、甘肃、四川、云南的藏区。他的要求太不现实了，美国应该劝达赖喇嘛退而求其次才对。

聪明的美国政治家，你们可以通过调查报告，知道全世界每个国家的人权情况，但没有必要以不友好的言行和立法干涉他国的内政，这绝对是对美国没有利的做法。美国要向世界推广人权的意向，首先必须以身作则，把自己的人权情况做到零缺点，树立良好的榜样，然后才以友好的态度引导别国向美国看齐，这才是推广人权的正确政策。

写于 2009 年 3 月 23 日

⊙洛杉矶女侨领黄惠珍驳斥达赖对西藏问题的谎言

Stop foolish action!

China military chiefs have accused a U.S. Navy Ship involved in a standoff near China's southern coast of spying. Meanwhile the U.S. led condemnation of China's treatment of its 6 million Tibetans voicing "deep concern" over human rights and calling Beijing to resume talk with the Dalai Lama.

These 2 incidents happened made so may people wonder why America is so foolish. While you need the whole world to cooperate with you specially the China to improve the financial crisis and to solve the economic recession yet at this moment you still send your spy ship to the door step of China and condemned the China on Tibet policy.

With these action and behavior you are obviously telling the world that you have never changed your "hegemony" attitude. At this moment you should be able to think, whether to please the 6 million Tibetan's or to gain the friendship of the 1.3 billion Chinese people. Whichever is more important to the peace of the world and to the greatest interest of the United States?

16th, March, 2009

停止愚蠢的行为

中国军事领导人指责美国一艘海军间谍船在中国南方海岸附近活动。同时美国谴责中国没有给予西藏 600 万人人权待遇，并敦促中国应该和达赖喇嘛进行谈判。

这两个意外事件同时发生，使很多人觉得美国很愚蠢，为什么正当美国需要和世界各国尤其是中国合作改善金融危机和拯救经济不景气的时候，派间谍船来中国口岸活动。又指责中国的西藏政策问题。肯定会得不偿失的。

从这些活动，人们可以很明显地看到美国的霸权主义还没有改变，在这个时刻美国应该懂得取悦 600 万藏人和争取 13 亿中国人的友谊。哪一方面重要？哪一方面更可以促进世界和平？哪一方面可以使美国可以获得更多的利益？

写于 2009 年 3 月 16 日

⊙ 中国驻旧金山副总领事就西藏问题举行记者会

The North Korea Nuclear Problem

In 2006 North Korea started nuclear test. She later agreed to dismantle its nuclear program during talks with China, Russia, South Korea, the US and Japan and reached a deal for shipment of fuel oil in return.

But the process has been stalled since last year by a dispute over how to verify North Korea's past nuclear activities. While waiting for North Korea to return to the negotiating table to solve the dispute, suddenly the North Korea ordered all nuclear experts in Korea to leave their country immediately. She declared that they are not going to take part in six party talks anymore and also will not follow any obligation that had been made and even threaten to start nuclear test again!

This sudden change could be in respond to the UN's condemnation to their rocket launch recently. In view of this America may not be able to stop the North Korea nuclear test.

In this circumstances America may have to consider the following suggestion in order to solve North Korea nuclear problems:

1. US to withdraw all Arm Forces station in South Korea in order to please majority of Korean people as well as to save billion of dollars per year of these military expenses for the US government.

2. To support and encourage South Korea to offer better term and conditions for reunion to North Korea. The reunion of German was a very good example for the U.S., the East German

朝鲜的核试问题

2006年朝鲜开始举行核试验，于2007年和中国、俄罗斯、韩国、美国和日本五国谈判后同意以汽油交换拆除核试验设备。

但拆除进程中，由于在如何检查朝鲜过去的核试活动问题上意见不同而停止下来。正当各方等待朝鲜回到谈判桌，以便解决有异见问题时，朝鲜却突然下令所有在朝鲜的国际核子专家，都必须马上离开朝鲜回国，并声言不仅要永远退出六方会谈，不再接受六方会谈有关协议的约束，而且还扬言要重新启动核试设施！

平壤当局这种突然的激烈举动可能是对联合国谴责其发射“卫星”后的反应。看情况，美国要朝鲜停止核试验的愿望可能很难实现了！

在这种情况下，美国也许应该考虑实行下列的建议，以便解决朝鲜的核试问题：

1. 美国把驻在韩国的军队全部撤走，以便取悦所有朝鲜、韩国对驻军不满的人民，也可以为美国在外驻军节省大量的费用。

2. 支持及鼓励韩国给朝鲜提供南北统一的良好条件，以德国为例子，当东德人民享受到统一后的资本主义生活，似乎就没有人喜爱原来的生活了，原东德人甚至当了德国

people after enjoying the capitalist life no one seem to be like old life anymore the powerful Germany leader Angela Merkel was an East Germany.

3. America should urge China to advise and convince North Korea to learn and adopt China open door and free market economy policy and support their reunion desire.

4. If the U.S. government would use the most effort to make the reunion of Korea successful and let the North Korea people have the equal chance to live with South Korea people peacefully they may forget their desire to have the nuclear weapons. This could be the best way to solve the problems.

21st, April, 2009

的女强人！

3. 美国应该请中国说服朝鲜学习中国的开放和实行自由市场的政策。并支持朝鲜和韩国的统一。

4. 如果美国能够认真尽力促成朝鲜和韩国的统一，使朝鲜人民能够和韩国人民享受同样的生活水准，他们便自然会把要拥有核弹的愿望放弃了！这是解决核试的更好办法。

写于 2009 年 4 月 11 日

⊙ 朝核问题各方反应

You cannot blame China for taking military action

Countries in the world were concerned that China and Taiwan might take military action, especially the ASEAN countries. They all advise Chinese to treasure peace and not to use military action to resolve problems,because the military action would not only impact the economies and trades between China and Taiwan, it would also affect peace and stability in the ASEAN region. Economic growth in the region would also be negatively impacted.

Since the ASEAN countries are so worried about the potential tension arised between China and Taiwan, why not cooperate and take a joint diplomatic action in mediating between the two sides to promote regional peace by finding viable solutions?

Everyone knows that before Lee Teng-hui's visit to the United States in June of 1995, cross-straits relationship was at ease. The reunion of China and Taiwan was looking promising through the frequent dialogue between senior officials of the two countries. Unfortunately, the United States did not take heed of China's objection and decide to accept Lee Teng-hui's "private visit." This resulted in Chinese officials believing that the U.S. was deliberately assisting Taiwan in establishing its international status and discouraging the idea of a reunion between China and Taiwan. As China deemed it necessary to prevent any potential for Taiwan to establish sovereignty, thus causing the cross-strait relationship became more tensed once again. Obviously the

不能怪中国采取军事行动

世界各国都担心海峡两岸会发生武装冲突，尤其是亚洲国家，都纷纷劝请中国以和为贵，不要以武力来解决问题，因为如果中国动武，不但会使海峡两岸的经济发展遭到破坏，亚洲的和平和稳定，也将会受到影响，各国的经济发展也可能会因此而放慢。

亚洲各国，既然如此担心两岸的纠纷会擦枪走火，为什么不联合起来，通过外交活动，为缓和海峡两岸的紧张关系担当调解角色，找出可行方案，为保护本区域的和平与安定而努力。

大家都知道，在李登辉于1995年6月访问美国之前，两岸风平浪静，和平统一的机会，通过双方“非官方”的不断接触，已经有了相当好的基础。可惜由于美国不顾中国的强力反对，故意让李登辉到美国作“私人访问”！因此中国政府认为美国此举是在助长台湾走向国际空间，有意背弃和平统一之道，中国有必要及时阻止这种趋势的发展。因此，两岸的关系便突然紧张起来！很明显地，这次两岸的交恶，美国是主要导火线！

对解决海峡两岸的政策，中国已经说得很清楚：只要台湾在言行上，不制造“两个中国”、“一中一台”和图谋

cross-straits's deteriorating relationship was due to the United States's permission of a private visit by President Lee Teng-hui.

China's position on resolving the cross-strait relationship has been made very clear: As long as Taiwan does not "create two Chinas" and declares its sovereignty, the union of China and Taiwan can be peacefully resolved over time.

We believe China is very aware that if China and Taiwan declare war, economic development in the two countries will be adversely affected. Economic growth and stability in Southeast Asia will also be directly impacted. No Asian countries would like to witness such a reality. That's why China has been very patient in dealing with Taiwan and the cross-straits relationship. Unless provoked, China will not take military action lightly. China has an ancient saying, "better to die with honour than to survive in disgrace." If Taiwan continues to insist on achieving sovereignty and opposes the One China policy, then it may be difficult to avoid what all Asians are most worried about, which is military action between China and Taiwan.

Taiwanese clearly understand that China is developing economy. China is aggressively promoting capitalism. Living standards and the degree of freedom continue to improve. The difference in living standards and freedom enjoyed by mainland Chinese and Taiwan are continually narrowing. Therefore, the different pace of economic development across the straits can no longer be the reason for not wanting to negotiate the reunification of China and Taiwan. China has said that it will not rely on the wealth created by Taiwan to subsidize and raise the standard of living in mainland China post-reunification. China is prepared to allow Taiwan to enjoy a similar level of freedom and autonomy as Hong Kong SAR. As long as reunification can be achieved in this

台湾独立，剩下的问题，都可以慢慢通过谈判和平解决的。

我们相信中国会清楚地知道：如果海峡两岸发生战争，不但双方的经济发展将遭受到严重破坏，东南亚的和平稳定及经济的增长，也将会直接间接受到影响，任何亚洲人都不喜欢看到这种局势的发生。因此，中国对台湾的不妥协态度，一忍再忍，若非万不得已，定是不会随便对台湾动武的，但中国有一句古训："宁为玉碎，不为瓦全"。台湾当局如果坚持采取分裂中国的立场，对抗一个中国的原则，那这场亚洲人不愿见到的灾难，恐怕最终还是难以避免。

台湾也清楚地知道：目前中国正在大力发展经济，人民的生活水准和自由程度，也已不断提高和改善。和台湾方面的差距，将会逐渐拉近。因此，两岸经济发展差距的问题，将不能作为不与中国谈判和平统一的理由。中国已经一再表明，两岸统一之后，不会利用台湾的财富去提高大陆人民的生活水平，中国也准备让台湾享有比香港更多更好的自治权。只要在名义上，能够早日达成"统一"的共识，中国是不会有过分要求的。

可惜台湾当局，对中国的和谈建议，不但不肯作出积极的反应，还一再作出触怒中国的言行：例如要花钱取得联合国席位，要美国修改《与台湾关系法》，要美国保证保护台湾的安全，要美国出售更多更好的武器，这些行为与活动，都说明了台湾没有诚意要和平统一。

form, China will not insist on overbearing conditions.

Unfortunately, in dealing with Chinese requests to discuss reunification, Taiwanese officials are not only unwilling to take concerted action, but continue to take actions that anger China: Spending resources to gain a seat at the United Nations; insisting that the United States amends its Taiwanese foreign policy; insisting on American protection; purchasing advanced U.S. military equipment. These actions and activities show that Taiwan is not sincere about peaceful reunification.

Therefore, we should not blame China for taking some military action and insisting that it will resolve the reunification issue through military action if needed. From the various incidents discussed above, we can clearly understand that the current tense cross-straits relationship is self inflicted by the Taiwanese policy. And the challenge faced in reaching a peaceful reunification between China and Taiwan is also due to American policy in dealing with Taiwan. An old Chinese saying states that to resolve an issue, we need the stakeholders to collaborate. Therefore, to avoid cross-straits military action, we need to put our hopes on the Taiwanese and the Americans.

If possible, the ASEAN countries should advise the Taiwanese authorities to face reality. Since the World (including the United States of America) has already recognized the one China policy, it will be impossible for Taiwan to achieve independence even if it exhausts the entire US$100 billion in its foreign reserves. To ensure that Asia continues to achieve its economic growth and to maintain cross-straits peace and stability, Taiwan should agree to negotiate terms of reunification and not to dream of "independence." This would be in the best interests of all Chinese people. Taiwan will become a province of China and

因此，我们不能怪中国采取一些军事行动，声言要以武力解决统一问题。从这些前因后果，我们可以清楚地看到，目前台湾海峡的紧张局势，是台湾自己造成的，而两岸和平统一所面临的重重困难，也是美国对台政策引起的。所谓解铃还须系铃人，要两岸避免军事冲突，我们应该寄希望于台湾和美国。

亚洲各国，有可能的话，应该协力劝请台湾当局必须面对现实。世界各国（包括美国）既然已经公认台湾是中国领土的一部分，若要脱离中国，争取独立，恐怕就算花尽了台湾库存的1000亿美元，也绝对办不到的。为了维持亚洲的继续繁荣发展，以及海峡和平与稳定的现状，不致被两岸的纷争所破坏，台湾应以中华民族为重，摒弃保留现状或争取独立的念头，以和为贵，尽早通过国际友好国家的协助和保证，向中国争取到表面“统一”，实际“独立”的最有利条件，使台湾完整地成为中国的宝岛，而宝岛上的人民，也将是比较富有及比较自由的中国人！有什么不好呢？

亚洲各国也许应该使用一点外交压力，劝请美国不要借口为保护他们在台湾的“利益”而不断在外交上、军事上及经济上支持台湾，明显地干预他国的内部纷争，使两岸关系火上加油，以致破坏两岸和平统一的希望。美国应该吸收越战的教训。出钱出力的结果是吃力不讨好的！如果再自不量力，再出钱出兵保护台湾，那将只有使其已亏

the people of the Taiwan province will be more affluent and enjoy greater freedom than people in mainland. Is that not a desirable outcome?

Perhaps ASEAN can place some foreign policy pressure to urge the U.S. not to continue to provide diplomatic, military and economic support to Taiwan in the name of protecting Taiwanese interests. U.S. Taiwanese policy continues to interfere with the internal issues of a third country, adds trigger to the cross-straits tension and dashes hope of reunification. America should learn from the Vietnam War that spending all the resources to intervene in other countries' internal issues will not result in the desired outcome. If the U.S. chooses to protect Taiwanese interests, it will undoubtedly dig a deeper hole in its US$390 billion budget deficit. It will also face difficulty in repaying its US$1.4 billion debt with the United Nation. Let Asia deal with its own problems and disputes. America should stay out of it to avoid the wrath of 1.3 billion Chinese. That would be a smart move.

7th, March 1996

(Published on 22nd, March, Lianhe Zaobao, editorial)

空的39000亿美元的国家赤字更加恶化！拖欠联合国的14亿美元的分担费也将难以还清！让亚洲人解决自己的纠纷，美国应该置身事外，以免种下被13亿中国人仇视的祸根，这才是聪明的做法。

写于1996年3月7日

刊于1996年3月22日《联合早报·言论版》

⊙ 台湾风光

On Reunification across the Taiwan Straits

Reading “conditions for ‘one country two systems’ has not prepared yet” issued by lecturer MaoYixin from the National University on Lianhe Zaobao commentary section, I thought her point of view was contradictive and not that pertinent: on one hand she approved the long-term interests reunification will bring to both sides of Taiwan Straits, while on the other hand, she thought reunification could not be realized under the circumstance of “one country two systems” at present but “one country one system” in the future. She advocated political critics should maintain a fair sense of responsibility while raised unreasonable queries about the definition of one China, giving rise to the discussion of “Amei incident”, a parrot embroidering the story on the purpose of stirring up trouble between the straits.

Lecturer Mao also used the suggestion of Senior Minister Lee Kuan Yew that mainland should not be over expected on Chen Shui-bian. This quoting would easily mislead readers to that Mr. Lee held the same opinion as hers: let Taiwan maintain current status! In fact, Minister Lee has always advised that the earlier the reunification was negotiated with CPC, the better conditions could be acquired by Taiwan. Minister Lee persuaded mainland “not to exert wrong judge on Chen Shui-bian too early”, while I believed his original idea was to advise mainland to spare time to Chen Shui-bian rather than take military action in too much hurry in order to resolve reunification problem between Taiwan straits.” Avoiding that the whole Chinese nation will pay a

谈两岸统一问题

读 6 月 30 日《联合早报》言论版由国大讲师茆懿心发表的《两岸仍未具备“一国两制”统一条件》，觉得她的言论有些矛盾和不中肯：一方面肯定统一对两岸的长远利益，另一方面又认为目前不能以“一国两制”达成统一条件，要等待将来在“一国一制”的条件下才谈统一。她一方面主张政治评论家应该采取比较公平的负责态度，另一方面却对一个中国的定义提出无理取闹的问题。炒“阿妹风波”的冷饭，人云亦云，添油加醋，唯恐两岸不乱！

茆讲师还借用了李光耀资政最近劝告大陆不要对陈水扁操之过急的意见。这样引用很容易误导读者，以为李资政亦和她的主张一样，让台湾保持现状！其实李资政向来都劝告台湾越早和大陆谈判，越可以取得更好的统一条件。李资政劝告大陆“不要太早对陈水扁下错误的结论”，相信他的本意是要劝告大陆多给陈水扁一点时间，不要太快采取军事行动，解决两岸统一问题，以免使“整个中华民族都将为这个错误付出沉重的代价”，和茆讲师的主张“等将来在‘一国一制’的条件许可下才谈和平统一”根本拉不上关系。未知茆讲师是真不懂，还是假不懂。

lot for this mistake" has no bearing on "peaceful reunification can only be talked about on the premise of 'one country one system'". It is not known that lecturer Mao really understood it or pretended she didn't.

Lecturer Mao, a native to Taiwan, must protect the interests of Taiwan and speak for Taiwanese, which is irreproachable. But as a lecturer in the National University of Singapore usually making remarks in local radio and newspaper with the support of many audiences and readers, taken that she could issue a quite positive comment on reunification between the Taiwan straits as mentioned in her article, persuading governors of both sides to cherish the peace and lead China to early reunification and wealth, she is a senior scholar worthy of respect from Chinese.

Lecturer Mao "accepted the impossibility of Taiwan independence, approved the long-term interests of reunification for two both sides, and advocated that both sides across the straits should overcome variety of difficulties to sign an agreement on the plan for reunification in a few years, maybe 30 years, maybe 15 years...". It is also known to mainland that conditions for reunification had not yet been presently conducive, so they advocate the transition agreement on the premise of "one country two systems" to accomplish complete reunification in 50 years, even longer than suggested by lecturer Mao! Therefore, "one country two systems" is the best cure for "sign an agreement on the plan for reunification in a few years". Mainland said: "on the premise of 'one China', everything can be negotiated." It obviously means: "Only require Taiwan people to identify themselves as Chinese, Taiwan is part of China." One China will be "administrated by all the Chinese." But there is no doubt the request to use "The Republic of China" to and the flag of Blue

茆讲师，原籍台湾，她要保护台湾的利益，要为台湾人说好话，原本无可厚非。但她既然是新加坡大学讲师，也经常在本地电台和报章发表评论，拥有不少听众和读者，对两岸统一问题，如果她能够和文里所说一样，采取比较正面的立论。劝说两岸领导人以和为贵，使中国能够早日统一，迈向富强之道，才不失为广大华人所尊敬的资深学者。

茆讲师既然“接受台湾独立的不可能性，也肯定统一对两岸的长远利益，并主张两岸应该克服各种困难，签订一个若干年后统一的协定，可能是30年，可能是15年……”，大陆知道目前谈统一的条件“水未到渠难成”，才主张以“一国两制”的办法来达成50年后才完全统一的过渡协定，比茆讲师所提的时间还长呢！所以“一国两制”才是“签订一个若干年后统一的协定”的最适合良方。大陆说：“一个中国下，什么都可以谈。”很明显地是说：“只要台湾人民肯定自己是中国人，台湾是中国的一部分”，一个中国“由所有中国人来管理”，但要用“中华民国”及青天白日旗的要求，当然是无理取闹。

站在中国的立场，台湾既然是中国领土的一部分，中国领导人当然可以说台湾选举“总统”是“闹剧”。如果在“一国两制”的协定下，台湾以同样民主方式选举“省长”，不但不会被视为“闹剧”，反而会成为被所有中国人都赞同的选举制度。茆讲师要中国总理尊重主张“台独”

Sky/White sun is unreasonable.

Standing at the position of China, since Taiwan is part of China's territory, governors of China are certainly qualified to say Taiwan president election was kind of "ridiculous drama". Under the framework of "one country two systems", election of "province governor" in the same democratic way would not be regarded as "ridiculous drama", but on the contrary considered an election system approved by all the Chinese. Lecturer Mao required China premiere to respect Taiwan politicians advocating Taiwan Independence, but is it possible? Isn't that unreasonable?

Lecturer Mao said, "HK people are busy with earning money, lack of political consciousness. China Communist Party's interference in many Hong Kong events made 'One country two systems' in Hong Kong work as a negative rather than positive example for Taiwan." But According to the report published in July 3rd issue of Hong Kong Yazhou Zhoukan: "As 3 anniversaries of Hong Kong Returning to China is approaching, Yazhou Zhoukan carry out the survey among representatives in various field of Hong Kong, inviting them to comment on the administration of Hong Kong SAR Government. Among 10 categories listed, 'relationship with the mainland' won the best score, the consecutive 3rd year record, which proved that the implementation of HK people governing HK under a high degree of autonomy' was widely recognized". Another report: in the last year, HK people carried out 6 demonstrations every day on average. These actual examples demonstrated to Taiwan people, under the policy of "one country, two systems", freedom of HK people is not necessarily less sufficient than Taiwanese, and their political consciousness is not weaker than Taiwanese. As for national affairs, it is for sure that the mainland has the

的台湾政治人物，有可能吗？对吗？

茆讲师说："香港人忙着赚钱，政治意识薄弱。中共对香港多项事件的干预使得香港的'一国两制'不但对台湾起不了示范作用，甚至可以说是提供了负面的示范。"但根据香港《亚洲周刊》7 月 3 日报道："在香港回归三周年之际，《亚洲周刊》再次向香港各界具代表性人物发出问卷，请他们对香港特区当局的施政作出评价。在所列的十个项目中，'与内地关系'一项获得最高分数，这是该项目连续第三年占据榜首，显示'港人治港，高度自治'的落实获得广泛认同"。又据报载：过去一年，香港每天平均有 6 次大小示威记录。这是以活生生的事实告诉台湾人，在"一国两制"之下，香港人的自由空间仍不比台湾差。政治意识也不比台湾人弱。至于国家大事当然要听大陆的意见。正如一家企业管理制度，重要事项的处理当然要由公司最高董事会决定，再交由经理层去执行，有什么不对？英国和美国在香港都拥有重大的经济利益，如果"一国两制"的实行有什么差错，他们还会以国家元首的地位接待董建华的到访吗？因此，香港的"一国两制"肯定会对台湾起示范作用的。

凡稍有见识或到过中国的人都知道，中国自上世纪 70 年代实行邓小平的经济政策以来，国家已经迈向现代化，人民生活水平也已经大大提高，早已变成有中国特色的社

power of decision. In management regulation of an enterprise, significant business should be directed by highest ranking board, and then carried out by management, but isn't it right? Both of the UK and the US own huge economic interests in HK, so if there is anything wrong with the implementation of "one country, two systems", will they welcome the visit of Tung Chee-hwa as heads of state? Thus, "one country, two systems" in HK will surely play an exemplary role for Taiwan.

It is known to the informed people or those had been to China, since 1970s when the economic policies of Deng Xiaoping started to carry out, the country has already advanced to modernization, the living standard of people has been improved considerably, and the social system has already turned to socialism with Chinese characteristics since long ago. Only some ignorant Taiwanese, misled by politicians, are still in the "fear of communist party", worrying about after peaceful reunification, would there be another Cultural Revolution? Lecturer Mao also said: "Our Taiwanese must doubt, have the consciousness and value of mainland people already walked out of that historical devastation?" It is pitiful that this question originated from a senior scholar. No doubt she thought that two sides have not yet satisfied the conditions for peaceful unification! US should not be misled by Taiwan separatist to avoid making a false move towards Taiwan.

3rd, July, 2000

会主义了。只有部分无知的台湾人，在政治家的误导下，才依旧犯着“恐共病”，担心和平统一之后，如果再来一次“文化大革命”怎么办？茆讲师同样说：“我们台湾人一定要质疑，大陆人的意识和价值观真的已经从那场历史浩劫中走出来了吗？”这种疑问出自一位资深学者，实在令人可惜又可叹。难怪她认为，两岸还达不到和平统一的条件！美国不应该受“台独”分子言论所误导，以免对台湾做出错误的决策。

写于 2000 年 7 月 3 日

⊙ 台北“京华城”雕塑寓意两岸统一

Another Word about the Reunification between the Taiwan Straits

Reading “Listen to the Voice of Taiwanese” published in the commentary section of April 15th issue of Lianhe Zaobao, author Shu Hongjun thought “feeling unfair about that no one has ever spoken for Taiwan so far”. He hoped people could listen more to the voice of Taiwanese rather than “only listen to the words of mainland”, and only after that they could reach fair judgment. It seemed his words pointed to my article “The Expectation of Overseas Chinese on across Taiwan Straits” is a partial statement written after listening to one-side words.

The author of article “Listen” said he was not a pro independent Taiwanese, but I am not that contented with his “voice”, so I had to write something to discuss with him about the issue of reunification between the straits, and hope it could change his prejudiced opinion on me.

It is known to every Singaporean that Singapore’s media has always being attentive and objective in the reports and comments on Taiwan Straits-related issues. For example, in this Taiwan presidential election, Zaobao reported impartially diverse words of different parties, which is obvious to all. Remarks of Democratic Progressive Party on Taiwan independence can be read without a word missing. Therefore, nobody spoke for Taiwan is not because people can not hear the voice of Taiwanese but the “voice” of Taiwan independence brought Chinese so much disappointment and repulsion, so few were willing to speak for Taiwan independence. Knowledgeable Singaporean would not

再谈两岸统一问题

读 4 月 15 日《联合早报》言论版《听听台湾人的声音》(以下简称《听》)，作者舒鸿君认为，“这么久以来未见到有人替台湾说一句话感到不平”。他要人们多听台湾人的声音，勿“单听大陆的说辞”，才能有公平的判断。字里行间似乎说 4 月 7 日拙文《海外华人对两岸的期望》是听了片面之词的偏袒言论。

《听》的作者说他不是“台独”分子，只是要为台湾人抱不平，但听完他的“声音”觉得有些不太顺耳，只好再动笔和他谈两岸的统一问题，希望能借此改变他对笔者的偏见。

每个新加坡人都知道新加坡媒体对两岸事件的报导和评论向来都是非常关注和客观的。例如：这次台湾“总统”选举，早报对不同党派不同言论都做了不偏不倚的报导，这都是有目共睹的事实。民进党“台独”的言论几乎都可以在本地报章一字不漏地读到。因此，没有人替台湾人说话的原因，并不是人们听不到台湾人的声音，而是“台独”的“声音”太令华人失望和反感了，才少有人肯为“台独”说好话。有广见的新加坡人是不会随便盲从的。而大多数

follow others slavishly. And most people support the peaceful reunification between the straits not because they only listen to the partial words of China mainland.

As an overseas Chinese, I advise two sides to cherish peace, and correct the erroneous opinion of Pro-independent Taiwanese, which should be accused of "interfering in internal affairs of other country"? It seems that Senior Minister Lee had ever said to Taiwan "It is unnecessary to take military actions to resolve Taiwan problem, and advise Taiwan to negotiate with China in order to earn better conditions for reunification". However, good advice is harsh to the ear. Taiwan authorities will not regret until overtaken by defeat. They thought they are free from troubles under the protection of Taiwan-US Security Treaty, adding to China is developing its own economy so they will certainly spare the rat to save the dishes, without destroying "Treasure Island" in impulse. However, Pro-independent Taiwanese please don't forget a Chinese saying: "It is better to die with honor than to live in infamy", which is not expected by millions of overseas Chinese. I hope Pro-independent Taiwanese will not be infatuated with the success of this election.

It is known to the informed people or those had been to China, since 1970s when the economic policies of Deng Xiaoping started to carry out, the country has already advanced to modernization, the living standard of people has been improved considerably, so how could incident of "leaving the peasants die of famine" described by Shu Hongjun occur? This is the outdated story repeated by Pro-independent Taiwanese to cheat Taiwan people, and will anybody believe it when it is brought up again in Singapore?

China spends money on buying weapons in order to prevent

人主张两岸应该和平统一，也不是听从了中国内地的片面之词。

站在海外华人的立场，劝告两岸以和为贵，纠正“台独”人士的错误观念，不应该算是“干涉人家的内政”吧？李资政也似乎曾经对台湾说过“中国可以不必动武，便能解决台湾问题，劝台湾越早和中国内地谈判越可以争取到越好的统一条件”。但忠言逆耳，台湾当局不见棺材不落泪！以为有台美安全条约的保护，便可以高枕无忧。何况中国正在发展自己的经济，必定会投鼠忌器，不会轻易将“宝岛”毁于一旦。可是，“台独”分子请别忘记中国有句格言“宁为玉碎，不为瓦全”，虽然这是千万海外华人所不愿见到的局面。希望“台独”分子不会被这次选举的胜利而冲昏了头脑。

凡稍有见识或到过中国的人都知道，中国自上世纪 70 年代实行邓小平的改革开放政策以来，国家已经迈向现代化发展，人民的生活水平也已经大大地提高了，怎么会有如舒鸿君所说“任由其农民贫死饿死”的事情发生呢？这是“台独”分子用以欺骗台湾人民的老调，在新加坡重弹会有人相信吗？

中国花钱买武器，还不是为了预防“台独”的背叛行为，台湾不是更可怜吗？有钱还难以买到心爱的武器呢！

因此，两岸如果能够悬崖勒马，早日和平统一，便可

the betrayal of pro-independent Taiwanese, so isn't Taiwan more pitiful? It is difficult for them to buy weapons they love even with money!

Therefore, if both sides can stop on the precipice to avoid fighting, and accomplish peaceful reunification early, weapons of both sides can be remained and work towards foreign powers. Japan may return Diaoyu Island automatically; disputes of Nansha Islands can be resolved quite reasonably, so there would be no need for US to mobilize too many troops to safeguard the security of Asia.

It is true that "Taiwanese don't think they need to return to the mainland" for living, but under the principle of "overcome impetuosity and exercise patience" raised by Lee Tung-hui, Taiwan enterprises still rush out to invest almost 40 billion dollars in the mainland, and the trade with mainland is more than 13 billion dollars every year. After "three exchanges", there should be a substantial increase in trade surplus without sharing these interests to Japan and Korea, the only choice left for Taiwan authorities is peaceful reunification, through which they can maintain this financial interests.

Pro-independent Taiwanese usually take Singapore as an example: since Singaporean Chinese are allowed to found Singapore as an independent country, why can not Taiwan Chinese found an independent Taiwan country and become Taiwanese?

It is not known whether these people really understand or they just pretend that they don't, independence of Singapore was realized after the separation sought initiatively by Malaysia to resolve the problem that two parties hold different political views.

Taiwan is part of China's territory legally, unless it is

将双方的武器完整保存下来，枪口一致对外。日本可能会自动送还钓鱼岛，南沙群岛的纠纷也可获得比较合理的解决，美国也不必再劳师动众来保护亚洲的安全了。

确实“台湾人并不觉得需要返回大陆”去居住，但台湾商家在李登辉“戒急用忍”的原则下，却仍争先恐后地到大陆去投资了近400亿美元，每年对大陆的贸易出超了130亿美元。“三通”之后出超数字肯定还会大幅度增加，这些肥水如果不想让它流到日本或韩国去，台湾当局唯有选择和平统一，才能够继续享有这些财经上的利益。

“台独”的人经常举新加坡为例子说：新加坡的华人既然可以成立新加坡国，做新加坡人，为什么台湾的华人就不能独立建“台湾国”做台湾人？

不知道这些人是真不懂，还是假不懂，新加坡是马来西亚主动要求脱离而独立建国，以便解决双方存有不同政见的问题。

而台湾在法理上是中国的领土，要独立，除非得到中国的同意。或者，叫世界各国包括美国在内，否定中国对台湾领土的拥有权。否则便应该尊重国际公法承认既成事实，退而求其次，所谓：“既然不能抗拒，便应该参与之”。早日和中国达成和平统一的优越条件，作为中国一个龙头省份，把台湾民主制度和发展经验在大陆继续发扬光大，让两岸人民共享荣华富贵，这才是上上之策。美国应该知

permitted by Chinese government it will never be independent, or through the way that all the countries in the world including US deny the ownership of China upon Taiwan. Otherwise the fact should be admitted with the respect of international public laws. Taking the next best way, now that you are not able to reject it, so why don't you join it? Making a concession with mainland for peaceful reunification with preferential conditions to be the top province, developing the democratic system and development experience of Taiwan in mainland, and enriching the wealth shared by the people between the Taiwan straits would be the optimal policy. US should be aware of Taiwan's role in acquiring the market of "freedom and democracy" in China for US after the peaceful reunification across the straits were accomplished.

17th, April, 2000

道，如果两岸能和平统一，台湾将可以帮美国在中国争取“自由民主”的市场。

写于 2000 年 4 月 17 日

⊙ 台北老兵反“独”促统

Expectation from Overseas Chinese on both Sides of Taiwan Straits

Millions of overseas Chinese are closely concerned with the future of China, especially about Taiwan issue, and furthermore hope both sides can cherish the peace. Reaching the agreement on conditions for reunification, each side can display its own advantages internally, develop separately, and externally take the same actions together to fight any unreasonable treatment from the foreign forces. The overseas Chinese could also be highly regarded by the world.

It is a pity that with the support of US government, Taiwan authorities has been refusing the suggestions of peaceful reunification from the mainland for so many years at the excuse of that majority of Taiwanese prefer to maintain the current status, so the accomplishment of peaceful reunification of the country expected by the Chinese all over the world has been delayed again and again.

Whereas, whoever started the trouble should end it. No matter how US government interfered, if Taiwan authorities can lead people to think about following problems and weigh the gain and loss, their erroneous views of maintaining current status and pursuing independence will be changed.

1. Taiwan is part of China's Territory.

Taiwan has been part of China from time immemorial, which was the fact recognized all over the world (including US). Therefore, Taiwan is the territory of all Chinese. Residents in

海外华人对两岸的期望

几千万海外华人都非常关心中国的前途，尤其对台湾问题，更深切希望两岸能够以和为贵。早日谈好统一的条件，对内可以各尽所长、分头发展，对外也可以行动一致，抗拒他国一切不合理的待遇。海外华人也会因此而让世人另眼相看。

可惜多年以来，台湾当局由于美国政府的撑腰，坚拒大陆和平统一的献议，理由是大多数台湾人都要保持现状，以致全世界华人热切盼望的祖国统一大业迟迟未能实现。

然而，解铃还须系铃人。不管美国政府怎么干预，只要台湾有关当局能够引导其人民对下列问题加以思考，衡量得失，便会改变其要保持现状、追求独立的错误观念。

1. 台湾是中国人的领土。

台湾自古便是中国的一部分，这是世界各国都承认的事实（包括美国在内）。因此，台湾也就是所有中国人的领土。而居住在台湾的人凡坚持自己是台湾人，而不是中国人者，在法理上都应该被列为非法居留的外国人，而要搞“台独”的人，则应该被视为要分裂祖国的叛徒，或是

Taiwan who claimed firmly to be Taiwanese rather than Chinese would be regarded as foreigners in illegal residence, and the pro-independent Taiwanese should be deemed as betrayers planning to split China, or the foreigners lusting after Chinese territory. These speeches or conducts are unacceptable by all Chinese people or overseas Chinese people. Thus, Taiwanese should abandon all the ridiculous wrong ideas wisely. Otherwise, please remember the severe warning from Chinese premier "who start Taiwan independence deserve bad ends".

2. US safeguard Taiwan — conduct of hegemony.

Now that US admitted Taiwan's part of China territory, but now and then warns China not to take military actions against Taiwan, otherwise it will take corresponding actions to protect Taiwan. Their overweening arrogance could intensify the hostility from Chinese to US and the resentment against Taiwan authorities' betrayal of national interests.

May I ask that if the Japanese immigrants who occupied a majority of population in Hawaii of US or Japanese descendents were bound to seek independence, would US government listen to this public opinion? If US government would take military actions to remove this unreasonable requirement of independence, would China send a warning to US with military dispatches to protect Hawaii? It is evident that US alleged to protect Taiwan overtly with the covert aim to use Taiwan as an unsunk aircraft carrier to hold down the development of China. Therefore, Taiwanese shall repent and avoid to be the sinner spitted by all Chinese people.

3. "Referendum" should be participated by All the Chinese.

The pro-independence Taiwanese daydream about that if Taiwan is kept in current status, "referendum" could be held at

对中国领土有野心的外国人。这是所有中国人及所有海外华人都不能容忍和接受的言行。因此，台湾人应该明智地抛弃这种几乎是幻想的错误观念，否则就请记住中国总理的厉声警告“谁要搞台湾独立，就没有好下场”。

2. 美国保台是霸权行为。

美国既然承认台湾是中国领土的一部分，却又不时警告中国不可对台湾动武，否则便会采取相应行动来保护台湾。这种嚣张霸道的心态将会加深中国人对美国的仇恨和对台湾当局出卖国家权益的不满。

试问：假如占美国夏威夷人口众多的日本移民和日裔要酝酿独立时，美国政府会顺从民意让他们独立吗？如果美国政府要以武力消除这种不合理的独立要求时，中国可以向美国发出同样的警告及可以出兵保护夏威夷吗？很明显的，美国政府口口声声要保护台湾，其实却是要利用台湾，将其作为一艘不沉的航空母舰，以便就近牵制中国的发展。因此，台湾人应该回头是岸，不要沦为民族的千古罪人，被所有华人所唾弃。

3. 所有中国人参与“公投”。

主张“台独”的人想得很美，以为把台湾保持现状，待时机成熟再举行“公投”，而当多数人赞成独立时，中国政府会在国际社会压力下顺从民意，让台湾独立。这也

a certain right moment, and when independence were favored by majority, China government would bow to public opinion and approve the independence of Taiwan under the pressure of the international society. This is a wrong idea.

The pro-independence Taiwanese should never forget that Taiwan is an inalienable part of China. If a referendum on the sovereignty of Taiwan is under the necessity of holding, all the Chinese people inside or outside Taiwan shall have the right to vote.

Therefore, Taiwanese could only have the right to select the party of Chinese for administration instead of to be a country with independent sovereignty at will. I am afraid all the Chinese people would be strongly against the latter.

4. Advantages to Maintain Current Status.

Taiwan seeks to maintain current status, rejecting "one country two systems", because Taiwanese are afraid of being gobbled up by CPC for the great disparity in strength after the reunification: politicians shall pursue the position as "boss of a small company" rather than "deputy boss of a big company". These are wrong and selfish ideas too.

In current status, though the general living standard of Taiwanese people is much higher than mainland, their wealth will not be appropriated by mainland people for sure. During at least another 50 years, no offending will occur under the supervision of international society. In 50 years, it is possible that mainlanders are even more wealthy than Taiwanese. Moreover, the new policies of mainland probably would sooner be more democratic and open than Taiwan's.

After the reunification, the title of Taiwan president would be changed, but serving as the governor of the wealthiest,

是错误的想法。

主张台湾独立的人，请不要忘记台湾是属于所有中国人的领土。要公投台湾的去留问题，应该让所有海内外中国人都参与投票才合理。

因此，台湾人只能选择由哪一党、哪一派的中国人来治理台湾，而不是台湾人说要独立，便可以独立成为一个自主国家。那样恐怕连所有海内外华人也都会极力反对的。

4. 保持现状有什么好处?

台湾要保持现状，不要“一国两制”，因为台湾人民担心统一后，势力悬殊会被共产党吞掉：政治家要当“小店的老板”，不要做“大公司的副手”。这也都是错误及自私的想法。

台湾目前的现状，虽然人民的平均生活比大陆富有，但绝对不会被大陆人民“共产”。至少 50 年内，在国际的保证下可以井水不犯河水。50 年后，有可能大陆人民已经比台湾人民更富有了。何况大陆本来的新政策也许很快会比台湾更民主、更开放。

统一后，台湾“总统”的名称可能会被更改，但当一个中国最富有、最发达、最民主自由的台湾特别省省长，在国内外到处被人羡慕，受人欢迎，总比目前到处吃闭门

developed and democratic special Taiwan province that were admired and welcome in China and foreign countries is much better than having the door slammed in the face everywhere. Furthermore, the Taiwan politicians who make contributions to the peaceful reunification of China will be the hero to all the Chinese people for his work in the national prosperity and solidarity.

5. Peaceful Reunification for Prosperity.

After the peaceful reunification, a great deal of military expenses would be saved for both parties. It is no need for Taiwan to spend unworthy money on buying off or aiding those trivial countries with an aim of building diplomatic relations. The money saved could be used for infrastructure construction, education and medical cares, making a better life for the people across the straits.

Under the circumstance free from internal disturbance and foreign aggression, Taiwan's rich experiences of financial and economic development and good international trade relations can be applied in coordination with vast territory and rich natural resources, which will enable China to catch up with western countries more rapidly and Chinese be certainly wealthier. The living situation of overseas Chinese would go up as the river rises without being bullied by others easily.

6. Great Chance for Taiwanese's Return to the Mainland.

China premier had ever said, as long as Taiwan are willing to accept the principle of "one county, two systems" to resolve the issues of reunification in peaceful way, anything could be put onto the negotiation table with concessions! Taiwan authorities could probably also take advantage of this chance to participate in political affairs in the mainland as a legal out-party. China may as well learn two-party system from US, and the successful

羹好得多。更重要的是凡领导促进和中国统一的台湾政治家，将是海外千万华人心目中国家民族大团结、大昌盛的功臣。

5. 和平统一国强民更富。

两岸和平统一后，双方将可节省大量军备费用。台湾也不必再花冤枉钱去收买或援助那些不关痛痒的国家，与其建立“邦交”。可以将省下来的钱，用在基建、教育及医疗方面，使两岸人民可以过更好的生活。

在没有内忧外患的环境之下，可利用台湾丰富的财经发展经验和良好的国际贸易关系，配合大陆的幅员辽阔及丰富资源，使中国可以更迅速地追上世界强国，人民也肯定会因而更富有。海外华人的处境自然会水涨船高，再不致被人任意欺负了。

6. 台湾人返回大陆良机。

中国总理说过，只要台湾愿意以“一国两制”方式和平解决统一问题，则什么都可以谈，可以让步！台湾当局也许可以利用这个机会，要求重新返回大陆参政，做一个合法的在野党。请中国学美国的两党制度，由胜选者轮流执政。相信所有中国人都会支持这个观念的。台湾的民主制度也许迟早会在大陆开花结果。希望台湾人不要放弃这个可以到大陆参政的良好机会。

party would come into power alternatively. I believe all Chinese people would support this idea. The democratic system of Taiwan would sooner or later blossom and bear fruit in the mainland. I hope Taiwanese would not abandon this chance to participate in political affairs in the mainland.

US should be aware of that if it could propel Taiwan to accept the condition of "one country, two systems", either US or Taiwan would obtain more interests in the end.

18th, March, 2000

美国应该知道，如果能够促进台湾接受“一国两制”的条件，那么美国无论在台湾还是大陆都将会获得更好的利益。

写于2000年3月18日

⊙ 美国南加州众多侨团发表《反对台湾“入联公投”联合声明》

A Unified China

ever-powerful China in the past

In history, the first unified China was founded 2,200 years ago by Qin Shihuang. After 10-year war, he annihilated six kindoms Han, Zhao, Yan, Wei, Chu and Qi in a row, ending the divisions that lasted for 500 years, and ruled ever-powerful China with the centralization of state power and multiplied nationalities.

grow to be a developing country

Nevertheless, why does China, a unified and extraordinarily powerful country 2,000 years ago, remain a developing country up to now?!

On the contrary, Japan, which was said in the legend to breed from 3,000 Chinese boys and girls, has become a strong economy today? The latecomer US even advanced by leaps and bounds to become the world's sole superpower merely 200 years after its founding. All these above merit the consideration of all the Chinese.

what keeps China away from prosperity?

No prosperity or no long-lasting prosperity was achieved during Chinese emperor dynasties and the first 40 years of Republic of China (Minguo), because governors in the past kept the door closed to outside world, arrogant with blindness, and concerned only the interests of local people within their own

一个统一的中国

昔日强大的中国

在中国历史上，第一个统一的中国，是由秦始皇於二千二百多年前所建立的。他当时历经十余年的战争，才先后消灭了韩、赵、燕、魏、楚、齐等六个诸侯国，结束了长达五百多年之久的分裂割据局面，而统治了一个中央集权，多元种族的强大的中国。

变为发展中国家

但是，一个二千多年前便已经统一而且非常强大的中国，为什么到现在仍是一个正在发展中的国家？

相反地，传说由中国三千童男童女所衍生的日本，现在却能成为世界的经济强国？而后来居上的美国，更能突飞猛进，建国只有短短二百多年，便能成为当今举世无双的超级强国。这是所有中国人都应该加以思考的问题。

不能强盛的原因？

中国历代皇朝，以至民国初期的 40 余年里，所以不

territory without caring about the future of the nation, without getting united to fight the enemy, without having great foresight and plan for the future, which led to a fraying society where people lived in misery and poverty, diplomacy was weak, and the country's international status was poor.

damages of the Civil War

When Japan ended the war of invading China 50 years ago, if Kuomintang(KMT) and Communist Party of China(CPC) avoided the civil war for the benefit of the nation's future, negotiated to adopt American way of administrating a country by two parties, abandoned prejudice and vied for the peaceful reunification with concerted efforts, it is believed that China today could have not only been capable to compete with western countries but also been strong enough to say "no" loud to any injustice in international affairs.

It is a pity that they both went to extremes. KMT relied on the strength of the US, but CPC was backed former Soviet Union, which resulted in damages in both sides. KMT retreated to Taiwan, and survived under the wings of the US over past 50 years, now the dream of reoccupying China's mainland shattered, and its ruling power, which Democratic Progressive Party(DPP) will substitute for sooner or later, on the verge of collapse.

Despite CPC liberated China's mainland, it took the party 30 years in power to learn that principles of distribution "from each according to his ability, and to each according to his needs" and "from each according to his ability, and to each according to his contribution" did not work. As a result, the prosperity of the country and people have been delayed decades, and this big mistake inflicted incalculable losses!

能强盛，或强盛不能持久的原因，是由于过去的统治者，对内闭关自守，盲目自大，只重视地方和族群的利益，不以国家民族的前途为重，对外不能团结一致，没有高瞻远瞩的世界观，以致造成内贫外弱，民不聊生，国无地位。

内战使两败俱伤

五十多年钱，日本结束侵略中国之后。如果当时的国民党和共产党，都能以国家民族前途为重，不要发生内战，双方协议采取美国式的两党治国政策，摒弃成见，共同为建设一个和平统一的中国而努力。相信目前的中国，不但可以与列强并驾齐驱，对任何不合理的国际事务都可以大声说“不”了。

可惜双方各走极端，国民党借助美国的力量，共产党则利用苏联的支持，结果造成两败俱伤。国民党只好退守台湾，五十多年来靠美国的保护而生存，现在不但没有希望可以反击大陆，连执政权利也危在旦夕，迟早将会被民进党所取而代之。

共产党虽然解放了整个大陆，但执政30多年以后才发觉“各尽所能，按需分配”或“各尽所能，按劳分配”的政策行不通，以致国家和人民在迈向富强的道路上被推迟了几十年，这是重大的错误，造成无可计量的损失！

The New Hope of Chinese

Fortunately, China adopted open new economic policy resolutely in mid 1970s, which greatly improved the living standard of Chinese people, and the wealth of nation thus began to grow, so that the new hope of Chinese was rekindled.

After the return of Hongkong and Macao to China's mainland, when will Taiwan come back to the embrace of motherland? When will the reunification be achieved? This is the issue all the Chinese concern and care about, since if Taiwan could peacefully return to China earlier, China would rank among the world's super powers sooner.

standpoints of reunification across Taiwan Straits

Chinese government has been stressing on that if Taiwan authorities admit there is only one China in the world and Taiwan is a special province of China, reunification conditions would be much easier than that of Hongkong, and any matter is negotiable. In "one country two systems", on the premise of "One-China", Taiwan will have a high degree of autonomy. Taiwan will not only keep its military force, but can also preserve its wealth and hold democratic election, and it is even negotiable to change the region's flag or name.

CPC offered so easy reunification conditions to make clear their stand for valuing the overall interests of the nation above everything else instead of claiming to be the winner, which is indeed commendable.

Unfortunately, Taiwan authorities rejected the "olive branch" from China's mainland on one pretext or another, alleging seemingly that due to extraordinary disparity in living standard across Taiwan straits and mainland had not yet developed

中国人的新希望

幸好70年代中期，中国终於果敢地实行了开放的新经济政策，大大改善了人民的生活，而国家的财富也开始有所增加，使中国人民又升腾起了新的希望。

随着香港，澳门回归中国之后，台湾什么时候能够回归？中国什么时候可以统一？这将是所有中国人及所有海外华人所关切和期盼的问题，因为台湾如能够早日和平回归祖国，将可使中国更快速地挤上世界强国之列。

两岸统一的立场

中国政府已经一再强调：只要台湾肯承认世界上只有一个中国，台湾是中国的一个特省，两岸统一的条件将会比香港宽松，什么都可以谈，“一国两制”，分而治之。台湾人不但可以保存自己的军事力量，也可以支配自己的财富，实行自己的民主选举政策，甚至改变国旗国号也都可以商量。

中共提出这样宽大的统一条件，肯定是以国家民族的利益为重，而不以胜者为王自居，确是难能可贵的献议。

可惜台湾当局却以种种理由拒绝接受大陆的“敬酒”，表面上说是因为两岸人民的生活水准仍非常悬殊，大陆还未能实行民主政策，台湾有80%以上的人主张维持现状，因此认为目前还不是谈到统一的时候，但骨子里却在寻求独立的可能性，不惜以大量金钱收买一些小国建立邦

a democratic system, above 80% of Taiwanese preferred to keep the normal status, so it is not the high time to talk about reunification. However, in actuality, they seek the chance to achieve Taiwan independence, and spare no money in buying off small countries to establish diplomatic relations; actively lobby US politicians to speak for Taiwan, and make disturbances to hamper Sino-US relations; spread continuously that a unified China would be a threat to Taiwan and the world; advocate that only when China is divided into 7 zones including Taiwan with each under independent autonomy, the threat could be dismissed. It is explicit of their stand "overt for reunification but covert for independence". Lee Teng-hui is already an incorrigible separatist, and his view fits in exactly with Japan's claim that China should be divided into 12 parts and suits the ambition of US to protect their own interests in Taiwan. This concept is beyond the ken of man indeed, so no wonder Chinese premier Zhu Rongji criticized Taiwanese for they "forget their own origin".

Taiwan should make no more mistakes

Singapore's Senior Minister Lee Kuan Yew made advices to Taiwan several years ago: the earlier the reunification was negotiated with CPC, the easier conditions could be acquired, and he also foresaw China could resume Taiwan without taking military action. Nevertheless, good advice is harsh to the ear, so Lee Teng-hui even made criticisms that Senior Minister Lee Kuan Yew did not understand the history of China

Taiwan authorities especially the leaders of KMT should not take it for granted that KMT can sit down and relax under the protection of US, for US just makes use of the relationship with Taiwan to achieve nothing more than gaining greater interests

交；积极游说美国政客，为台湾说好话做好事，千方百计制造妨碍中美关系发展的事故；一再散布一个统一的中国会对台湾和世界造成威胁的言论；提出将中国分成七个区块，包括台湾在内独立自治，这样才不会造成对世界的威胁。清清楚楚地确认了他“明统暗独”的立场。李登辉这些无药可救的分裂主义者，正中了以前日本要把中国支解为 12 块的主张，及美国要维护他们在台湾利益的目的。真是“匪夷所思”的构想，难怪朱镕基要大骂“台独”份子“数典忘祖”。

台湾别一错再错

新加坡李光耀资政早在几年前便已忠告台湾，越早与中共谈判统一的事，越可以取得更好的条件，他也预言，中国不必动用武力，便能够达到收回台湾的目的。但忠言逆耳，李登辉甚至为此而批评李资政太不懂中国的历史！

台湾当局尤其是国民党的领导人别以为有了美国的保护便可以高枕无忧，美国只是要利用与台湾的关系作为向中国大陆索取更高利益的筹码而已。当中国被逼不惜对美国付出任何代价以换取完成统一中国大业时，台湾便可以不必流血而回归祖国了。

台湾当局，尤其民进党领导人，也别以为有众多的台湾人要维持台湾现状，便可通过利用民意牌，而取得执政权。

from China's mainland. When China is forced to pay any cost to US in exchange for the great cause of complete reunification, Taiwan will return to China without bloodshed.

Taiwan authorities especially the leaders of DPP should not take it for granted that DPP can play on many Taiwanese's wish of maintaining current status to seize the power.

Actually the public opinion in Taiwan is full of narrow localism, which is the result of the long-term misdirection of Taiwan pro-independence activists. As long as conscientious politicians guide Taiwanese and tell them straightforwardly: only when China is unified, an unexampled prosperity could be achieved, and China could be capable to be on a par with super powers. The military expenses saved after the reunification could be used for the improvement of education and living standard for across-straits people. On the premise of "One China", wealth of Taiwan remains belonging to Taiwan, and Taiwanese could not only maintain current living conditions, but also have stronger security guarantee abroad given by the country. Therefore, only the leader who can muster up his courage to advocate the reunification with China's mainland will be regarded as a leader that really loves Taiwan.

KMT leaders shall abandon personal kindness and enmity, taking emphasis on the future of the nation and holding the bravery of "how can you catch tiger cubs without entering the tiger's lair?" Don't miss another chance of cooperating with CPC in jointly administrating the country. Before the power is seized by DPP, KMT should accept CPC's policy of "One Country Two Systems", and register in provinces of China's mainland for participation in management of political affairs. CPC could also hold campaign in Taiwan, helping KMT eliminate the wrong

其实台湾的民意是存在着狭隘的地方主义，是受“台独”分子不断误导的结果。只要有良知的政治家予以开导，直截了当地告诉台湾人：只有一个统一的中国，国家才会更加富强，才不会被列强所随意欺凌。统一后省下的军事费用，可以使两岸人民受着更好的教育，过着更富裕舒适的生活。在“一国两制”的政策之下，台湾的财富，还是属于台湾人的，台湾人不但可以维持不变的生活现状，在国外的安全，也可以获得国家更有力的保护。因此，敢于公开主张，应该和大陆统一的领导人，才是真正爱台湾的领导人。

国民党领导人应该抛弃个人恩怨，以国家民族前途为重，抱着不入虎穴焉得虎子的勇敢精神，别再错过可以与中共争取联合执政的另一次机会，赶在政权未被民进党夺去之前，接受中共的“一国两制”政策，让国民党可以在大陆各省注册参政。共产党也同样可到台湾活动，协助国民党将民进党的错误立场消灭。

统一是大势所趋

台湾前“行政院”院长郝伯村说“两岸关系中，台湾方面本来拥有相当的主导性，不过已逐渐流失”。他指出当初美国提出三个“不”时，两岸关系可以有包括台独在内的和平解决选项。去年克林顿与大陆联合发表新三不之后，就只剩下主张统一的唯一途径！

standpoints of DPP.

reunification is an inexorable trend

Former premier of Taiwan Executive Court Hau Pei-tsun said, "Taiwan originally take the initiative in across-straits relations, but they have gradually lost it." He pointed out when the US came up with "Three-No" policy, there are peaceful solutions for across-straits relations including Taiwan Independence. Since Clinton and China's mainland jointly launched new "Three-No" policy last year, the only solution left is reunification!

But what he thought "In next generation, that is, after 20 or 30 years, it would be the time to solve the issue concerning sovereignty" seems to be so wishful thinking!.

After the sovereignty of Macau was transferred, Beijing would be bound to intensify the pursuit of peaceful reunification back by the threat of force and the way of negotiation. Chinese leaders all hope to accomplish the great cause of across-straits reunification during their terms. Moreover, international situation such as rampancy of US hegemony, continuous expansion of NATO, and the rising of Chinese exclusion force in Japan made all the Chinese realize that both sides of the straits should accomplish peaceful reunification to build a strong nation so that our people can be free from being humiliated. The lastest poll held by Mainland Affairs Council showed: The proportion of Taiwanese favoring the reunification has risen. It proved that reunification is an inexorable trend which may be accomplished in 3 or 5 years. If America do not purpose to stop it.

Published in Paris "Europe Times" of 22nd, June, 1999

但他认为“下一代也就是二,三十年左右，应该是处理两岸主权问题的恰当时机”未免太一厢情愿了!

继澳门主权移交后，北京势必会加紧以战逼和，以谈逼统。中国当今领导人，肯定希望在任期内能够完成两岸统一的千秋大业。加之上美国的霸权主义到处横行，欧洲北约组织的不断扩大，日本排华势力的抬头等国际局势，中国人及海外华人都感受到两岸应该早日和平统一，才能建设强大的祖国，人民才能免于被欺凌。最近陆委会民意调查显示，台湾民众倾向两岸统一的比例也上升了。可见要求中国统一是大势所趋，也许三至五年内便可以实现了。如果美国不从中阻止的话。

刊于 1999 年 6 月 22 日巴黎《法华报》

⊙ 中华人民共和国庆祝建国 60 周年国庆联欢晚会

Asian Solve Their Disputes by Themselves

Some governors in our country proposed that "American force should remain in Asia playing positive role. Because China would be the most powerful military power in Asia, and there would be no balanced power to counterbalance China, only US at the back and Japan can work as balanced power."

But the Defense Secretary of Malaysia Syed Hamid said: "The rising of China could make another military superpower in the world, which is an inevitable fact." However, he did not regard "China as a threat to the security of Asia and the world". On the contrary, he affirmed "China would make contributions to regional security and peace".

It is believed that US is welcomed by all the Asian people to remain in Asia playing a leading role to help develop economy and promote development of science and technology. However, if US wants to play a role as international police to safeguard the peace and stability of Asia, it would be going for wool and come home shorn! The chaos would come after the "aid"! During Vietnam War and Korean War, US delivered money and force resulted in making the two nations separated and inflicting countless suffering on the people of these two countries, which left Asian poor war record!

Before Taiwan President Lee Teng-hui visited US, the situation between the Taiwan straits was stable, and the path towards peaceful reunification had been underway through constant non-governmental contacts. Nowadays, the situation

亚洲人解决自己的纷争

我国有些领导人主张："美国的势力应该继续留在亚洲，扮演积极角色。因为中国将成为亚洲最大的军事强国，亚洲将没有平衡的力量可以对付中国，只有在美国成为靠山加上日本才能算是平衡的力量。"

但大马国防部长赛哈密却说："中国将崛起成为世界的另一个军事强国，这是无可避免的事实。但中国不会对本区域及世界的安全构成威胁。"相反地，他也肯定"中国会对区域安全及和平做出贡献"。

要美国留在亚洲扮演协助发展经济，以及促进科技的领导角色，相信所有亚洲人都会表示欢迎的。但要美国在亚洲充当国际警察，维护亚洲的和平和稳定，则恐怕会弄巧成拙！越帮越乱！越战和韩战，美国出钱出力，结果只有把这两个国家变成一边一国，使这两个国家的人民受到无穷尽的伤害，给亚洲人留下了恶劣的印象！

台湾李登辉"总统"访问美国之前，两岸风平浪静，和平统一之路，已通过民间的接触在不断地探索。现在，海峡两岸的紧张局势，正是由于美国准许李登辉到美国访问造成的。因为中国认为美国此举是在主张台湾争取国际承认，背弃了和平统一之道，必须及时阻止这种趋势。

between the Taiwan straits was due to that US permitted the visit of Taiwan president Lee Teng-hui. Because China regarded this move signaled that US supported Taiwan to seek world wide recognition, which abandoned the path toward the peaceful reunification, and this tendency should be prevented instantly.

Therefore, we hope there would be no war between the Taiwan Straits, so at to avoid a high price paid by both sides and the passive influence in security and development of other countries in southeast Asia. We should urge US to pursue "one China" policy, abandon interfering with stand on Taiwan issues without adding fuel to the fire, and let China and Taiwan solve their problems by themselves. We should also persuade US to stop wantonly interfering in the internal affairs of Asian countries at the excuse of protecting their "interests" in Asia. The disputes of Asia would be solved by themselves. The infestation of US in the Middle East has sown the seeds of hostility of 1 billion Muslims, and would US intend to be the enemy of 1.3 billion Chinese people? Remaining in Asia, US should be helpful to its peace.

28th, Feb, 1996

因此我们希望台湾海峡不致燃起战火，以避免双方付出高昂的代价，影响到东南亚其他国家的安定和发展。我们应该劝请美国遵行“一个中国”的政策，对台湾问题采取不干预的立场，不要火上加油，让海峡两岸和平解决自己的问题。我们更应该劝请美国，不要借口保护他们在亚洲的“利益”而随便干涉亚洲各国的内政，应该让亚洲人解决自己的纷争。美国在中东的横行，已种下了被 10 亿穆斯林仇视的祸根，难道还要与 13 亿中国人为敌吗？美国要留在亚洲，就应该对亚洲的和平有所帮助。

写于 1996 年 2 月 28 日

⊙ 亚洲议会和平协会第三届年会闭幕